Exploring Austrian Cuisine: A Culinary Journey Through the Heart of Europe

VOLODYMYR RYBAIEV

Table of contents

Introduction to Austrian Cuisine 4
   Historical Background 4
   Regional Influences 6
   Key Ingredients in Austrian Cuisine 9
   Culinary Traditions in Austrian Cuisine 11
Appetizers and Small Bites 14
   Wiener Schnitzel Bites 14
   Käsespätzle (Cheese Noodles) 17
   Kartoffelsalat (Potato Salad) 20
   Liptauer Cheese Spread 23
   Tafelspitzsulz (Cold Beef Aspic) 25
Soups and Stews 28
   Gulaschsuppe (Goulash Soup) 28
   Leberknödelsuppe (Liver Dumpling Soup) 34
   Frittatensuppe (Pancake Soup) 37
   Krautfleckerl (Cabbage Pasta) 40
Main Courses 42
   Wiener Schnitzel (Breaded Veal or Pork Cutlets) 42
   Schweinsbraten (Roast Pork) 44
   Rindsrouladen (Beef Roulades) 47
   Tafelspitz (Boiled Beef with Horseradish) 50
   Kärntner Kasnudeln (Carinthian Cheese Noodles) 53
Side Dishes 57
   Erdäpfelsalat (Potato Salad) 57
   Rotkraut (Red Cabbage) 59
   Knödel (Dumplings) 62
   Semmelknödel (Bread Dumplings) 64

Sauerkraut 67
Vegetarian and Vegan Options 69
    Gemüsestrudel (Vegetable Strudel) 69
    Eierschwammerlgulasch (Chanterelle Mushroom Goulash) 73
    Krautfleckerl (Cabbage Pasta) 76
    Spinatknödel (Spinach Dumplings) 78
    Kürbiscremesuppe (Pumpkin Cream Soup) 81
Desserts and Pastries 83
    Apfelstrudel (Apple Strudel) 83
    Sachertorte (Sacher Torte) 86
    Linzer Torte (Linzer Cake) 90
    Topfenstrudel (Quark Strudel) 93
    Mozartkugeln (Mozart Balls) 96
Beverages 99
    Glühwein (Mulled Wine) 99
    Almdudler (Austrian Herbal Soda) 101
    Wiener Melange (Viennese Coffee) 104
    Sturm (Young Wine) 106
    Schnapps 108
Special Occasion Recipes 111
    Weihnachtsgans (Christmas Goose) 111
    Osterpinze (Easter Bread) 114
    Silvesterkrapfen (New Year's Eve Doughnuts) 117
    Heiliger Abend Suppe (Christmas Eve Soup) 120
    Osterlamm (Easter Lamb Cake) 123
Conclusion 125
    The Enduring Allure of Austrian Cuisine 125

Encouragement to Explore and Enjoy Austrian Cooking
.... 127

Introduction to Austrian Cuisine

Historical Background

Austria's culinary heritage is a tapestry woven from the threads of its rich history, geographical diversity, and cultural influences. To truly appreciate Austrian cuisine, it is essential to delve into the historical roots that have shaped it into what it is today.

1. Ancient Foundations

- Austria's culinary history traces its origins to ancient times, with evidence of early human settlements in the region dating back to the Paleolithic era.
- Celtic and Illyrian tribes inhabited the area, leaving their mark on the culinary landscape with the use of grains, game meats, and foraged herbs.

2. Roman Influence

- The Romans, who conquered the region in the 1st century BC, introduced new ingredients such as wine, olive oil, and various herbs and spices.
- Roman culinary techniques, including the art of sausage-making and the use of sauces, had a lasting impact on Austrian cuisine.

3. Medieval Era

- The Middle Ages brought about feudalism, with a clear distinction between the diets of nobility and peasants.
- Monasteries played a crucial role in preserving and refining culinary traditions, as they were centers of learning and gastronomy.

4. Habsburg Dynasty

- The Habsburg Dynasty, which ruled over Austria for centuries, significantly influenced the country's cuisine. They expanded their empire across Europe, introducing Austrian ingredients and dishes to different regions.
- The import of exotic ingredients from the New World, such as potatoes and maize, further enriched Austrian cuisine.

5. Coffee Houses and Pastries

- Vienna became renowned for its coffee houses during the 17th century. These coffee houses became hubs of intellectual and social activity, serving as places where people gathered to discuss politics, art, and literature.
- The tradition of pairing coffee with exquisite pastries, including the famous Sachertorte and Apfelstrudel, was born during this era.

6. Austrian-Hungarian Empire

- The Austro-Hungarian Empire, which spanned from the late 19th century until the end of World War I, brought together a diverse range of culinary influences from regions like Bohemia, Hungary, and Slovenia.
- The empire's multi-ethnic composition contributed to the variety of dishes found in Austrian cuisine today.

7. Post-World War II and Modernization

- After World War II, Austria faced a period of rebuilding and economic growth. This era witnessed changes in dietary habits, with the emergence of convenience foods and international influences.

- Austrian cuisine adapted to meet the demands of a more modern lifestyle, yet it also continued to preserve its traditional dishes.

8. Contemporary Austrian Cuisine

- In recent years, Austrian cuisine has experienced a renaissance, with chefs embracing both traditional and innovative approaches.
- Locally sourced and seasonal ingredients, as well as sustainable and organic practices, have become key trends in modern Austrian cooking.

Understanding the historical context of Austrian cuisine not only deepens one's appreciation for its flavors but also reveals the resilience of a culinary tradition that has evolved over centuries. As we embark on this culinary journey through Austria, we will explore the enduring traditions and vibrant flavors that make Austrian cuisine a treasure worth savoring.

Regional Influences

Austria's diverse landscape, featuring mountains, valleys, lakes, and fertile plains, has given rise to a rich tapestry of regional cuisines. Each Austrian province boasts its own unique culinary traditions, ingredients, and specialties. Exploring these regional influences provides a deeper understanding of Austria's gastronomic heritage.

1. Vienna (Wien)

- The capital city, Vienna, is a culinary epicenter known for its elegant coffee houses, pastry shops, and refined cuisine.
- Famous dishes: Wiener Schnitzel, Apfelstrudel, Sachertorte.

- Coffee culture: Vienna is celebrated for its coffee culture, with traditional coffee houses serving up Viennese coffee specialties like Melange and Einspänner.

2. Lower Austria (Niederösterreich)

- Located to the northeast of Vienna, Lower Austria boasts fertile farmlands and vineyards.
- Dishes: Tafelspitz (boiled beef), Wachauer Marillenknödel (apricot dumplings), and Grüner Veltliner wine.
- Agricultural products: Lower Austria is famous for its apricots, asparagus, and wine production.

3. Styria (Steiermark)

- Styria, in southeastern Austria, is known for its lush green landscapes and forests.
- Signature dish: Steirischer Backhendl (fried chicken).
- Pumpkin seed oil: Styria is renowned for its high-quality pumpkin seed oil, used in salads and dressings.

4. Salzburg

- The birthplace of Mozart and a region of stunning alpine beauty.
- Specialties: Salzburger Nockerl (sweet soufflé), Kasnocken (cheese dumplings), and Mozartkugeln (Mozart balls).
- Alpine cuisine: Salzburg features hearty alpine fare, often incorporating dairy products and game meats.

5. Tyrol (Tirol)

- Nestled in the Austrian Alps, Tyrol is known for its picturesque mountain villages and outdoor activities.
- Dishes: Tiroler Gröstl (pan-fried potatoes and meats), Kaiserschmarrn (shredded pancake), and Speck (cured ham).
- Dairy and cured meats: Tyrol's cuisine makes extensive use of dairy products and locally produced ham.

6. Carinthia (Kärnten)

- Carinthia is a region of pristine lakes and forests in southern Austria.
- Specialties: Kärntner Kasnudeln (cheese noodles), Reindling (yeast cake with cinnamon and raisins), and fish from Lake Wörthersee.
- Freshwater cuisine: Carp and trout are popular in the local diet due to the abundance of lakes.

7. Upper Austria (Oberösterreich)

- Upper Austria is characterized by rolling hills and the Danube River.
- Dishes: Linzer Torte (Linzer cake), Stelze (pork knuckle), and Mühlviertler Hasenöhrl (potato dumplings).
- Linzertorte: Linz, the regional capital, is famous for the Linzer Torte, a traditional Austrian cake.

8. Burgenland

- Burgenland, in eastern Austria, is known for its vineyards and unique cuisine.
- Dishes: Esterházytorte (Esterházy cake), Pannonian fish dishes, and Uhudler wine.

- Wine region: Burgenland is one of Austria's top wine-producing regions, offering a variety of red and white wines.

9. Vorarlberg

- The westernmost region of Austria, Vorarlberg, is situated in the Alps.
- Specialties: Käsknöpfle (cheese dumplings), Riebel (cornmeal dish), and mountain cheese.
- Alpine cuisine: Vorarlberg's cuisine reflects its alpine surroundings, featuring hearty and warming dishes.

Exploring the regional influences of Austrian cuisine allows us to appreciate the diversity and depth of this culinary tradition. Each region contributes its unique flavors and culinary heritage, making Austrian cuisine a true reflection of the country's geographical and cultural richness.

Key Ingredients in Austrian Cuisine

Austrian cuisine is characterized by a mix of hearty, alpine-inspired dishes and elegant, urban creations. These dishes often feature a selection of key ingredients that have played a pivotal role in shaping the nation's culinary identity. Here are some of the key ingredients commonly used in Austrian cuisine:

1. Pork: Pork is a staple in Austrian cuisine, often used in various forms, including sausages, schnitzel, and roast pork (Schweinsbraten). It's a versatile meat that features prominently in many traditional dishes.

2. Veal: Veal is another popular meat in Austrian cooking, especially in the iconic Wiener Schnitzel, a breaded and fried veal or pork cutlet. It's valued for its tender texture and mild flavor.

3. Beef: Beef is used in several Austrian dishes, such as Tafelspitz (boiled beef) and Rindsrouladen (beef roulades). High-quality beef is prized for its richness and depth of flavor.

4. Game Meat: In regions like Tyrol and Styria, game meats like venison, wild boar, and hare are frequently incorporated into dishes, reflecting the hunting traditions of the alpine areas.

5. Potatoes: Potatoes play a central role in Austrian cuisine, appearing in various forms like Erdäpfelsalat (potato salad), Kartoffelsuppe (potato soup), and Kartoffelknödel (potato dumplings).

6. Dumplings: Dumplings, or "Knödel," come in various types, such as Semmelknödel (bread dumplings) and Kärntner Kasnudeln (cheese-filled pasta dumplings). They are often served as side dishes.

7. Cabbage: Cabbage, particularly red cabbage (Rotkraut) and sauerkraut, is a common accompaniment to many Austrian meals. It adds a tangy and crunchy element to the plate.

8. Dairy Products: Austria is known for its high-quality dairy products. Cream, butter, and various cheeses, such as Emmentaler and Bergkäse, are used in numerous recipes, especially in alpine cuisine.

9. Apples: Apples are a versatile fruit used in both sweet and savory dishes. They are a key ingredient in Apfelstrudel (apple strudel) and various desserts.

10. Nuts: Nuts, especially hazelnuts and walnuts, are often included in Austrian desserts and pastries, providing a delightful crunch and flavor.

11. Herbs: Fresh herbs like parsley, chives, and dill are frequently used to add flavor and freshness to dishes. Caraway seeds are also a common spice.

12. Paprika: Paprika, though more commonly associated with Hungarian cuisine, is used in Austrian dishes like Gulaschsuppe (goulash soup) to add depth and color.

13. Pumpkin: Pumpkin and pumpkin seed oil, a specialty of Styria, feature in soups, salads, and various dishes, adding a unique nutty flavor.

14. Flour: Wheat flour is a fundamental ingredient for Austrian bread, pastries, and the delicate strudel pastry.

15. Wine: Austria is known for its wine production, and local wines, both red and white, are often used in cooking and enjoyed as accompaniments to meals.

These key ingredients, along with the influence of neighboring countries and Austria's own unique culinary traditions, come together to create the diverse and flavorful world of Austrian cuisine. Whether you're savoring a traditional dish in a cozy mountain hut or indulging in a Viennese coffeehouse, these ingredients are sure to be at the heart of your culinary experience.

Culinary Traditions in Austrian Cuisine

Austrian cuisine is steeped in tradition, reflecting the country's rich history and cultural diversity. These culinary traditions are an integral part of Austrian life, celebrated in daily meals, festivals, and family gatherings. Here are some of the culinary traditions that have shaped Austrian cuisine:

1. Coffee House Culture (Kaffeehauskultur):

- Austria is famous for its coffee house culture, which dates back to the 17th century in Vienna.
- Coffee houses are more than just places to enjoy a cup of coffee; they are cultural institutions where

people gather to discuss literature, politics, and the arts.

- Traditional coffee specialties like Melange, Einspänner, and Kapuziner are often accompanied by a slice of cake or a pastry.

2. Kaffee und Kuchen (Coffee and Cake):

- It is customary in Austria to take a break in the afternoon for "Kaffee und Kuchen," or coffee and cake.
- Families and friends come together to enjoy a leisurely afternoon with a selection of homemade or patisserie-bought cakes and pastries.

3. Sunday Family Meals:

- Sunday lunches and dinners are significant in Austrian culture, where families often gather for a hearty meal.
- Roasts, schnitzels, and traditional dishes like Tafelspitz are commonly served on these occasions.

4. Advent and Christmas Traditions:

- The Advent season is a magical time in Austria, marked by Christmas markets, holiday decorations, and special treats.
- Traditional Advent wreaths are lit each Sunday leading up to Christmas, and families enjoy festive meals together.
- Christmas Eve is celebrated with a feast, featuring dishes like Weihnachtsgans (Christmas goose) and various cookies and sweets.

5. Fasching and Carnival Celebrations:

- Fasching, or Carnival season, is celebrated with colorful parades, masquerade balls, and sweet treats.
- Traditional pastries like Krapfen (doughnuts) and Faschingskrapfen are enjoyed during this time.

6. Heuriger Tradition:

- In wine-producing regions like Vienna and Burgenland, the Heuriger tradition involves visiting local wine taverns to sample young wines and enjoy rustic, homey dishes.
- The atmosphere is informal, and visitors can often expect live music and conviviality.

7. Alpine Cuisine:

- In the alpine regions of Austria, there is a strong tradition of hearty mountain cuisine.
- Alpine huts (Almhütten) offer dishes like Kaiserschmarrn (shredded pancake) and Kasnocken (cheese dumplings) to hikers and skiers.

8. Seasonal and Local Ingredients:

- Austrian cuisine places a strong emphasis on using seasonal and locally sourced ingredients.
- Many families have gardens or visit local markets to obtain fresh produce.

9. Culinary Festivals and Events:

- Austria hosts numerous culinary festivals and events throughout the year, celebrating regional specialties and traditional dishes.
- Examples include pumpkin festivals in Styria and wine festivals in the wine regions.

10. Gasthaus Tradition:

- Gasthäuser, traditional inns or taverns, have been central to Austrian dining for generations.

- These establishments serve classic Austrian dishes in a warm and welcoming atmosphere.

These culinary traditions have been passed down through generations, preserving the authenticity and cultural significance of Austrian cuisine. Whether it's savoring a slice of Sachertorte in a Viennese coffeehouse or sharing a festive meal with family during the holidays, these traditions continue to define the Austrian culinary experience.

Appetizers and Small Bites
Wiener Schnitzel Bites

Wiener Schnitzel is a beloved Austrian classic, consisting of breaded and fried veal or pork cutlets. *Wiener Schnitzel Bites* offer a delightful twist on this iconic dish, making it

14

perfect for parties, appetizers, or a quick snack. Here's how to prepare this delicious Austrian treat:

Ingredients:

For the Schnitzel Bites:

- 1 pound (450g) veal or pork cutlets, thinly sliced into bite-sized pieces
- Salt and freshly ground black pepper, to taste
- 1 cup all-purpose flour, for dredging
- 2 large eggs, beaten
- 2 cups fine breadcrumbs (preferably fresh)
- Vegetable oil, for frying
- Lemon wedges, for serving

For the Potato Salad:

- 1 pound (450g) waxy potatoes (e.g., Yukon Gold), boiled and diced
- 1 small red onion, finely chopped
- 2 tablespoons fresh chives, chopped
- 3 tablespoons vegetable oil
- 2 tablespoons white wine vinegar
- Salt and freshly ground black pepper, to taste

Instructions:

For the Schnitzel Bites:

1. **Prep the Meat:** Season the veal or pork pieces with salt and pepper on both sides.

2. **Dredge in Flour:** Place the flour in a shallow dish. Dredge each meat piece in the flour, shaking off any excess.

3. **Dip in Eggs:** Dip the floured meat into the beaten eggs, ensuring they are well-coated.

4. **Coat with Breadcrumbs:** Finally, coat the meat with the breadcrumbs, pressing gently to adhere.

5. **Heat Oil:** In a large skillet, heat about 1/2 inch of vegetable oil over medium-high heat. To check if the oil is hot enough, drop a breadcrumb into it; if it sizzles and turns golden, the oil is ready.

6. **Fry Schnitzel Bites:** Carefully place the coated meat pieces in the hot oil, making sure not to overcrowd the pan. Fry until they are golden brown and crispy on both sides, about 2-3 minutes per side.

7. **Drain and Serve:** Remove the Schnitzel Bites from the oil and place them on paper towels to drain any excess oil. Serve hot with lemon wedges.

For the Potato Salad:

1. **Prepare Potatoes:** Boil the potatoes in salted water until tender but still firm. Drain and let them cool.

2. **Make Dressing:** In a large bowl, whisk together the chopped onion, chives, vegetable oil, white wine vinegar, salt, and black pepper.

3. **Dice Potatoes:** Once the potatoes are cool enough to handle, peel and dice them into bite-sized pieces.

4. **Combine and Chill:** Add the diced potatoes to the dressing and toss to coat evenly. Let the potato salad chill in the refrigerator for at least 30 minutes to allow the flavors to meld.

5. **Serve:** Serve the potato salad alongside the Wiener Schnitzel Bites as a refreshing and tangy side dish.

Enjoy your homemade Wiener Schnitzel Bites with a squeeze of fresh lemon juice and a side of potato salad for a true taste of Austria's culinary heritage!

Käsespätzle (Cheese Noodles)

Käsespätzle is a beloved comfort food in Austria, often compared to macaroni and cheese but with its own unique Alpine twist. This dish combines tender egg noodles, rich melted cheese, and crispy fried onions for a hearty and satisfying meal. Here's how to make it:

Ingredients:

For the Spätzle:

- 2 cups all-purpose flour
- 3 large eggs
- 1/2 cup water

- 1/2 teaspoon salt
- 1/4 teaspoon ground nutmeg (optional)
- 2 tablespoons butter, for later use

For the Cheese Sauce:

- 2 cups grated Emmentaler or Gruyère cheese (or a combination)
- 1 cup grated Austrian Bergkäse (if available, or use more Emmentaler/Gruyère)
- 1 cup whole milk
- 2 tablespoons butter
- Salt and freshly ground black pepper, to taste

For the Fried Onions:

- 2 large onions, thinly sliced
- 2 tablespoons vegetable oil
- Pinch of salt

Instructions:

For the Spätzle:

1. **Make the Dough:** In a large mixing bowl, combine the flour, eggs, water, salt, and nutmeg (if using). Mix until a smooth, elastic dough forms. It should be thicker than pancake batter but not as thick as traditional pasta dough.
2. **Boil Water:** Bring a large pot of salted water to a boil.
3. **Form the Spätzle:** There are several ways to form Spätzle. You can use a Spätzle press, a colander with large holes, or simply a knife and a cutting board. The traditional method is to scrape small,

irregular-shaped noodles directly into the boiling water.

4. **Cook the Spätzle:** Once the Spätzle float to the surface (usually within 2-3 minutes), remove them with a slotted spoon and transfer them to a colander to drain.

5. **Melt Butter:** In a large skillet, melt 2 tablespoons of butter over medium-high heat. Add the cooked Spätzle and sauté for a few minutes until they start to turn golden. Remove from heat and set aside.

For the Cheese Sauce:

1. **Prepare Cheese Mixture:** In a saucepan, melt 2 tablespoons of butter over medium heat. Add the grated cheeses and milk. Stir constantly until the cheeses are fully melted, and the mixture is smooth. Season with salt and black pepper to taste.

For the Fried Onions:

1. **Fry the Onions:** In a separate pan, heat 2 tablespoons of vegetable oil over medium-high heat. Add the thinly sliced onions and a pinch of salt. Fry until the onions are golden brown and crispy, stirring occasionally. Remove from heat and drain on paper towels.

Assemble and Serve:

1. **Combine:** Preheat your oven to 350°F (175°C). In a large baking dish, layer half of the sautéed Spätzle, followed by half of the cheese sauce. Repeat the layers with the remaining Spätzle and cheese sauce.

2. **Bake:** Place the baking dish in the oven and bake for about 15-20 minutes, or until the Käsespätzle is bubbling and the top is lightly golden.

3. **Finish with Fried Onions:** Just before serving, sprinkle the crispy fried onions over the top of the Käsespätzle.

4. **Serve:** Serve hot as a comforting and indulgent Austrian dish.

Käsespätzle is the ultimate comfort food, perfect for cold winter nights or whenever you're craving a rich and cheesy delight. Enjoy!

Kartoffelsalat (Potato Salad)

Kartoffelsalat is a beloved side dish in Austrian cuisine, and there are many regional variations throughout the country. This recipe presents a classic Austrian potato salad that features a tangy, flavorful dressing with a hint of sweetness. It pairs wonderfully with grilled meats or as a picnic dish.

Ingredients:

For the Potato Salad:

- 2 pounds (about 1 kg) waxy potatoes (e.g., Yukon Gold or red potatoes)
- 1 small red onion, finely chopped
- 2 tablespoons fresh chives, chopped
- 3-4 slices of bacon, cooked and crumbled (optional, for added flavor)
- Salt and freshly ground black pepper, to taste

For the Dressing:

- 1/2 cup vegetable oil (such as sunflower or canola oil)
- 1/4 cup white wine vinegar
- 1 tablespoon Dijon mustard
- 1 teaspoon granulated sugar
- 1 teaspoon salt
- 1/2 teaspoon black pepper
- 1/2 teaspoon caraway seeds (optional, for a traditional touch)

Instructions:

1. **Boil the Potatoes:** Place the whole unpeeled potatoes in a large pot of cold, salted water. Bring the water to a boil and cook the potatoes until they are fork-tender but not falling apart, typically 15-20 minutes depending on the size of the potatoes.

2. **Cool and Peel:** Drain the potatoes and let them cool until you can handle them comfortably. Then, peel the potatoes while they are still warm. This makes it easier for the potatoes to absorb the dressing.

3. **Slice the Potatoes:** Slice the peeled potatoes into 1/4-inch (0.6 cm) thick rounds and place them in a large salad bowl.

4. **Prepare the Dressing:** In a separate bowl, whisk together the vegetable oil, white wine vinegar, Dijon mustard, sugar, salt, black pepper, and caraway seeds (if using). Taste the dressing and adjust the seasonings according to your preference.

5. **Dress the Potatoes:** Pour the dressing over the sliced potatoes while they are still warm. This allows the potatoes to absorb the flavors better. Gently toss to coat the potatoes evenly with the dressing.

6. **Add Onions and Chives:** Add the finely chopped red onion, fresh chives, and crumbled bacon (if using) to the potato salad. Toss everything together until well combined.

7. **Chill and Serve:** Cover the salad and refrigerate it for at least 2 hours to allow the flavors to meld. Before serving, give it a final toss and adjust the seasoning if needed.

8. **Serve:** Serve your Austrian Kartoffelsalat as a side dish at picnics, barbecues, or alongside grilled meats or sausages. It's also a great accompaniment to schnitzel or other traditional Austrian dishes.

This Austrian Kartoffelsalat offers a delightful combination of creamy potatoes and a zesty dressing, creating a dish that's both comforting and refreshing. Enjoy!

Liptauer Cheese Spread

Liptauer is a traditional Austrian cheese spread with a rich, tangy, and slightly spicy flavor. It's often served as an appetizer or snack, typically enjoyed with fresh bread, pretzels, or crackers. This recipe allows you to make this delightful spread at home.

Ingredients:

- 8 ounces (about 225g) cream cheese, softened
- 4 tablespoons unsalted butter, softened
- 2 tablespoons sweet paprika
- 1 teaspoon caraway seeds, crushed
- 2 tablespoons finely chopped red onion
- 2 teaspoons Dijon mustard
- 2 teaspoons capers, finely chopped
- 2 teaspoons anchovy paste (optional, but traditional)
- 2 teaspoons Worcestershire sauce

- 1 teaspoon white wine vinegar
- 1/4 teaspoon cayenne pepper (adjust to taste)
- Salt and freshly ground black pepper, to taste
- Chopped fresh chives or green onions, for garnish (optional)

Instructions:

1. **Soften the Cream Cheese and Butter:** Allow the cream cheese and unsalted butter to come to room temperature for about 30 minutes. This makes them easier to mix.

2. **Crush Caraway Seeds:** Crush the caraway seeds using a mortar and pestle or by placing them in a plastic bag and gently pounding them with a rolling pin. This releases their aromatic flavor.

3. **Prepare the Spread:** In a mixing bowl, combine the softened cream cheese, softened butter, sweet paprika, crushed caraway seeds, finely chopped red onion, Dijon mustard, capers, anchovy paste (if using), Worcestershire sauce, white wine vinegar, and cayenne pepper.

4. **Mix and Season:** Using a fork or a hand mixer, blend all the ingredients together until well combined and smooth. Taste the spread and adjust the seasoning with salt and freshly ground black pepper to your liking. You can also add more cayenne pepper if you prefer a spicier kick.

5. **Chill and Serve:** Transfer the Liptauer cheese spread to a covered container and refrigerate for at least 1 hour before serving. Chilling allows the flavors to meld and intensify.

6. **Garnish and Serve:** Just before serving, garnish the Liptauer with chopped fresh chives or green onions,

if desired. Serve it with slices of fresh bread, pretzels, or crackers.

7. **Enjoy:** Spread it generously on your chosen accompaniment and savor the creamy, tangy, and slightly spicy flavors of this Austrian classic.

Liptauer Cheese Spread is a delightful addition to any appetizer spread or party platter. Its bold flavors and creamy texture make it a favorite among cheese lovers and a wonderful taste of Austrian cuisine.

Tafelspitzsulz (Cold Beef Aspic)

Tafelspitzsulz is a classic Austrian dish that combines the flavors of boiled beef, aromatic spices, and a savory aspic jelly. It's typically served cold and makes for a refreshing appetizer or light meal. Here's how to prepare this traditional Austrian dish:

Ingredients:

For the Beef and Broth:

- 2 pounds (about 900g) beef shank or round, with bone
- 1 onion, peeled and quartered
- 1 carrot, peeled and chopped
- 1 celery stalk, chopped
- 1 leek, cleaned and chopped
- 2 cloves garlic, smashed
- 2 bay leaves
- 8-10 whole peppercorns
- Salt, to taste
- Water

For the Aspic:

- 2 cups beef broth (reserved from cooking the beef)
- 2 teaspoons unflavored gelatin
- Salt and freshly ground black pepper, to taste

For Serving:

- Freshly grated horseradish or horseradish sauce
- Chopped fresh chives or parsley
- Sliced radishes (optional)

Instructions:

For the Beef and Broth:

1. **Boil the Beef:** Place the beef shank or round in a large pot and add enough water to cover it. Bring the water to a boil, then reduce the heat to a gentle simmer.

2. **Add Vegetables and Spices:** Add the onion, carrot, celery, leek, garlic, bay leaves, whole peppercorns, and a pinch of salt to the pot.

3. **Simmer:** Let the beef simmer uncovered for about 2 to 2.5 hours, or until it becomes tender and easily pulls apart.

4. **Strain and Reserve Broth:** Remove the beef from the broth and set it aside to cool. Strain the broth through a fine sieve or cheesecloth, reserving 2 cups of the broth for the aspic. You can use the remaining broth for soups or other dishes.

For the Aspic:

5. **Bloom Gelatin:** In a small bowl, sprinkle the gelatin over 1/4 cup of cold water. Allow it to sit for about 5 minutes to bloom.

6. **Warm Beef Broth:** In a saucepan, gently warm the 2 cups of beef broth over low heat. Do not boil.

7. **Dissolve Gelatin:** Once the broth is warm, add the bloomed gelatin and stir until it completely dissolves. Season the mixture with salt and black pepper to taste.

8. **Assemble and Chill:** In a mold or individual serving dishes, place some of the cooled, shredded beef. Pour the warm beef broth mixture over the beef until it's fully covered.

9. **Chill:** Refrigerate the Tafelspitzsulz for at least 4 hours, or until the aspic has set and the dish is cold.

To Serve:

10. **Unmold and Garnish:** To serve, carefully unmold the aspic onto a serving platter or individual plates. Garnish with freshly grated horseradish or

horseradish sauce, chopped fresh chives or parsley, and sliced radishes if desired.

11. **Enjoy:** Slice and savor the delicious, cold beef aspic, which is a delightful blend of flavors and textures.

Tafelspitzsulz is a wonderful example of traditional Austrian cuisine, combining the tender goodness of beef with the savory appeal of aspic. It's a refreshing and elegant dish that's perfect for special occasions or as an appetizer on a warm day.

Soups and Stews
Gulaschsuppe (Goulash Soup)

Gulaschsuppe, or Goulash Soup, is a hearty and flavorful dish that hails from Hungary but is beloved throughout Austria and Central Europe. This warming soup features tender chunks of beef, paprika, and a medley of vegetables. It's perfect for cold winter days or when you crave a comforting bowl of soup. Here's how to make it:

Ingredients:

- 1.5 pounds (about 700g) beef stew meat (such as chuck or round), cut into 1-inch cubes
- 2 tablespoons vegetable oil
- 2 onions, finely chopped
- 2 cloves garlic, minced
- 2 tablespoons sweet paprika
- 1 teaspoon smoked paprika (optional, for a smoky flavor)
- 1 teaspoon caraway seeds
- 2 bay leaves
- 2 red bell peppers, chopped
- 2 carrots, peeled and chopped
- 2 potatoes, peeled and diced
- 1 tomato, chopped
- 4 cups beef broth
- 1 cup water
- Salt and freshly ground black pepper, to taste
- Sour cream or yogurt, for garnish (optional)
- Chopped fresh parsley, for garnish

Instructions:

1. **Sear the Beef:** In a large soup pot, heat the vegetable oil over medium-high heat. Add the cubed beef and sear it until it's browned on all sides. Remove the beef from the pot and set it aside.

2. **Saute Onions and Garlic:** In the same pot, add the chopped onions and minced garlic. Sauté them until they become soft and translucent, about 5 minutes.

3. **Add Spices:** Stir in the sweet paprika, smoked paprika (if using), caraway seeds, and bay leaves. Cook for another 2 minutes, stirring constantly to prevent burning.

4. **Return Beef and Add Vegetables:** Return the seared beef to the pot. Add the chopped red bell peppers, carrots, potatoes, and tomato. Mix everything together.

5. **Pour in Broth and Water:** Pour in the beef broth and water, ensuring that all the ingredients are well submerged. Season with salt and freshly ground black pepper to taste.

6. **Simmer:** Bring the mixture to a boil, then reduce the heat to low. Cover the pot and let the soup simmer for about 1.5 to 2 hours, or until the beef is tender and the vegetables are cooked through.

7. **Adjust Seasoning:** Taste the soup and adjust the seasoning with more salt and pepper, if needed.

8. **Serve:** Ladle the Goulash Soup into bowls. If desired, garnish each serving with a dollop of sour cream or yogurt and a sprinkle of chopped fresh parsley.

9. **Enjoy:** Serve your homemade Gulaschsuppe with crusty bread or rolls for a hearty and satisfying meal.

This Goulash Soup is a comforting and flavorful dish that captures the essence of Central European cuisine. Its rich flavors and tender chunks of beef make it a true comfort food classic.

Kaspressknödel Suppe (Cheese Dumpling Soup)

Kaspressknödel Suppe is a delightful Austrian soup featuring crispy cheese dumplings served in a flavorful broth. This comforting dish is perfect for warming up on chilly days or enjoying as a satisfying appetizer. Here's how to make it:

Ingredients:

For the Cheese Dumplings (Kaspressknödel):

- 1 1/2 cups stale bread cubes (white or whole wheat)
- 1/2 cup milk
- 1 1/2 cups shredded mountain cheese (e.g., Bergkäse or Gruyère)
- 1/2 cup finely grated Parmesan cheese
- 1 small onion, finely chopped
- 2 cloves garlic, minced
- 2 tablespoons fresh chives, chopped

- 2 large eggs
- Salt and freshly ground black pepper, to taste
- Butter or vegetable oil, for frying

For the Soup:

- 6 cups vegetable or beef broth
- 1 onion, finely chopped
- 1 carrot, peeled and chopped
- 1 celery stalk, chopped
- 1 leek, cleaned and chopped
- 2 cloves garlic, minced
- 1 bay leaf
- 2 tablespoons butter
- Salt and freshly ground black pepper, to taste
- Chopped fresh parsley, for garnish

Instructions:

For the Cheese Dumplings (Kaspressknödel):

1. **Soak Bread Cubes:** Place the stale bread cubes in a bowl and pour the milk over them. Let them soak for about 10 minutes until softened.
2. **Prepare Dumpling Mixture:** In a large mixing bowl, combine the soaked bread cubes, shredded mountain cheese, grated Parmesan cheese, finely chopped onion, minced garlic, chopped fresh chives, eggs, salt, and freshly ground black pepper. Mix until all ingredients are well incorporated.

3. **Shape Dumplings:** Using your hands, shape the mixture into golf ball-sized dumplings. You can make them slightly flattened for easier frying.

4. **Fry Dumplings:** Heat a skillet over medium-high heat and add a bit of butter or vegetable oil. Fry the dumplings until they are golden brown and crispy on both sides. Set them aside.

For the Soup:

5. **Sauté Vegetables:** In a large soup pot, melt the butter over medium heat. Add the finely chopped onion, carrot, celery, leek, and minced garlic. Sauté until the vegetables become tender and aromatic, about 5-7 minutes.

6. **Add Broth:** Pour in the vegetable or beef broth and add the bay leaf. Bring the soup to a gentle simmer and let it cook for about 10-15 minutes to allow the flavors to meld.

7. **Remove Bay Leaf:** Remove the bay leaf from the soup.

8. **Serve:** To serve, place a few crispy cheese dumplings (Kaspressknödel) into individual soup bowls. Ladle the hot broth over the dumplings. Garnish with chopped fresh parsley and freshly ground black pepper.

9. **Enjoy:** Serve your Kaspressknödel Suppe hot, and enjoy the delicious combination of crispy cheese dumplings and flavorful broth.

This Cheese Dumpling Soup is a delightful Austrian dish that showcases the country's love for both cheese and comfort food. It's a great addition to your repertoire of warming soups.

Leberknödelsuppe (Liver Dumpling Soup)

Leberknödelsuppe is a traditional Austrian soup featuring savory liver dumplings served in a flavorful broth. This hearty dish is popular in Austria and is often enjoyed as a comforting appetizer or light meal. Here's how to make it:

Ingredients:

For the Liver Dumplings (Leberknödel):

- 1/2 pound (about 225g) chicken or calf's liver, finely chopped
- 1 small onion, finely chopped
- 2 tablespoons butter
- 1/2 cup breadcrumbs
- 1/4 cup milk
- 1 large egg
- 2 tablespoons fresh parsley, finely chopped
- 1/2 teaspoon salt

- 1/4 teaspoon white pepper
- A pinch of nutmeg (optional)
- Flour, for dusting

For the Soup:

- 6 cups beef or vegetable broth
- 1 onion, finely chopped
- 1 carrot, peeled and chopped
- 1 celery stalk, chopped
- 1 leek, cleaned and chopped
- 2 cloves garlic, minced
- 1 bay leaf
- 2 tablespoons butter
- Salt and freshly ground black pepper, to taste
- Chopped fresh parsley, for garnish

Instructions:

For the Liver Dumplings (Leberknödel):

1. **Saute Onions and Liver:** In a skillet, heat 2 tablespoons of butter over medium heat. Add the finely chopped onion and sauté until it becomes translucent. Add the chopped liver and cook for a few minutes until it's no longer pink in the center. Remove from heat and let it cool.

2. **Prepare Bread Mixture:** In a small bowl, combine the breadcrumbs and milk. Let them soak for a few minutes until the breadcrumbs absorb the milk.

3. **Blend Liver Mixture:** In a food processor, combine the cooked liver and onion mixture, soaked

breadcrumbs, egg, chopped fresh parsley, salt, white pepper, and nutmeg (if using). Pulse until you have a smooth mixture.

4. **Form Dumplings:** Dust your hands with flour to prevent sticking. Form the liver mixture into small dumplings, about the size of a walnut. Roll each dumpling in your hands to shape it.

5. **Boil Dumplings:** Bring a large pot of salted water to a simmer. Carefully add the liver dumplings to the simmering water. Cook them for about 15 minutes, or until they float to the surface and are cooked through. Remove them with a slotted spoon and set them aside.

For the Soup:

6. **Sauté Vegetables:** In a large soup pot, melt 2 tablespoons of butter over medium heat. Add the finely chopped onion, carrot, celery, leek, and minced garlic. Sauté until the vegetables become tender and aromatic, about 5-7 minutes.

7. **Add Broth:** Pour in the beef or vegetable broth and add the bay leaf. Bring the soup to a gentle simmer and let it cook for about 10-15 minutes to allow the flavors to meld.

8. **Remove Bay Leaf:** Remove the bay leaf from the soup.

9. **Serve:** To serve, place a few liver dumplings (Leberknödel) into individual soup bowls. Ladle the hot broth over the dumplings. Garnish with chopped fresh parsley and freshly ground black pepper.

10. **Enjoy:** Serve your Leberknödelsuppe hot, savoring the delicious combination of savory liver dumplings and flavorful broth.

Leberknödelsuppe is a comforting and hearty Austrian soup that showcases the country's culinary heritage. It's a unique and flavorful dish that's perfect for those who appreciate the rich, savory flavors of liver.

Frittatensuppe (Pancake Soup)

Frittatensuppe is a classic Austrian soup known for its delicate, thinly sliced pancakes (crepe-like strips) floating in a clear broth. This light and flavorful soup is often enjoyed as a comforting appetizer or a light meal. Here's how to make it:

Ingredients:

For the Pancakes (Frittaten):

- 2 large eggs
- 1 cup all-purpose flour
- 1 cup milk
- A pinch of salt

- Vegetable oil, for frying

For the Soup:

- 6 cups beef or vegetable broth
- 1 small carrot, peeled and sliced into thin rounds
- 1 small leek, cleaned and sliced into thin rounds
- 1 small celery stalk, sliced into thin rounds
- 1 small onion, finely chopped
- 1 bay leaf
- 2 tablespoons butter
- Salt and freshly ground black pepper, to taste
- Chopped fresh chives or parsley, for garnish

Instructions:

For the Pancakes (Frittaten):

1. **Prepare Batter:** In a mixing bowl, whisk together the eggs, all-purpose flour, milk, and a pinch of salt until you have a smooth, lump-free batter.

2. **Cook Pancakes:** Heat a non-stick skillet over medium-high heat and add a small amount of vegetable oil to coat the bottom. Pour a ladleful of the batter into the hot skillet, swirling it to create a thin, even pancake. Cook for about 1-2 minutes until the edges start to lift, then flip and cook for another 1-2 minutes until lightly golden. Repeat this process with the remaining batter, adding more oil to the pan as needed. Once cooked, transfer the pancakes to a plate and let them cool.

3. **Roll and Slice:** Once the pancakes have cooled, roll them up and slice them into thin strips, creating the "Frittaten."

For the Soup:

4. **Sauté Vegetables:** In a large soup pot, melt the butter over medium heat. Add the finely chopped onion, carrot rounds, leek rounds, celery rounds, and the bay leaf. Sauté the vegetables until they become tender and aromatic, about 5-7 minutes.

5. **Add Broth:** Pour in the beef or vegetable broth and bring the soup to a gentle simmer. Let it simmer for about 10-15 minutes to allow the flavors to meld. Season with salt and freshly ground black pepper to taste.

6. **Remove Bay Leaf:** Remove the bay leaf from the soup.

7. **Serve:** To serve, ladle the hot soup into bowls and add a generous portion of the sliced pancakes (Frittaten) to each bowl.

8. **Garnish:** Garnish your Frittatensuppe with chopped fresh chives or parsley for a burst of color and flavor.

9. **Enjoy:** Serve your Frittatensuppe hot and savor the delicate, savory pancakes in the flavorful broth.

Frittatensuppe is a simple yet satisfying Austrian soup that's both delicious and comforting. It's perfect for those looking for a light and flavorful dish with a touch of Austrian culinary tradition.

Krautfleckerl (Cabbage Pasta)

Krautfleckerl is a classic Austrian comfort dish that combines pasta with sautéed cabbage and onions, resulting in a hearty and flavorful meal. This dish showcases the simplicity of Austrian cuisine and is loved for its satisfying flavors. Here's how to make it:

Ingredients:

- 8 ounces (about 225g) wide egg noodles or pasta (such as fettuccine or pappardelle)
- 1 small head of green cabbage, thinly sliced
- 1 large onion, thinly sliced
- 3 tablespoons vegetable oil or butter
- 1 teaspoon caraway seeds (optional, for traditional flavor)
- 1 teaspoon paprika
- Salt and freshly ground black pepper, to taste
- Chopped fresh parsley, for garnish (optional)

Instructions:

1. **Cook the Pasta:** Bring a large pot of salted water to a boil. Cook the pasta according to the package instructions until it is al dente. Drain the pasta and set it aside.

2. **Prepare the Cabbage and Onions:** While the pasta is cooking, heat the vegetable oil or butter in a large skillet or frying pan over medium-high heat. Add the thinly sliced cabbage and onions. If using, sprinkle the caraway seeds over the cabbage and onions. Sauté them until they become tender and start to brown, about 10-15 minutes.

3. **Season with Paprika:** Once the cabbage and onions are tender, sprinkle paprika evenly over the mixture. Stir to coat the cabbage and onions with the paprika, allowing it to bloom and infuse the dish with its flavor. Season with salt and freshly ground black pepper to taste.

4. **Add the Cooked Pasta:** Add the cooked and drained pasta to the skillet with the sautéed cabbage and onions. Toss everything together, ensuring that the pasta is well coated with the cabbage and onion mixture. Cook for an additional 2-3 minutes to heat the pasta through.

5. **Garnish and Serve:** Transfer the Krautfleckerl to serving plates. If desired, garnish with chopped fresh parsley for a burst of color and flavor.

6. **Enjoy:** Serve your homemade Krautfleckerl hot and savor the delightful combination of pasta and savory cabbage and onions.

Krautfleckerl is a wonderful representation of Austrian comfort food, highlighting the delicious simplicity of its cuisine. It's a satisfying dish that's perfect for a cozy meal on a chilly evening.

Main Courses
Wiener Schnitzel (Breaded Veal or Pork Cutlets)

Wiener Schnitzel is one of Austria's most famous dishes, featuring thin, breaded, and fried veal or pork cutlets. This classic Austrian recipe is cherished for its simplicity and deliciousness. Here's how to make it:

Ingredients:

- 4 veal or pork cutlets (about 4 ounces each), pounded to about 1/4-inch thickness
- Salt and freshly ground black pepper, to taste
- 1 cup all-purpose flour, for dredging
- 2 large eggs
- 2 cups fine breadcrumbs (preferably from white bread)

- Vegetable oil, for frying
- Lemon wedges, for serving
- Parsley sprigs, for garnish (optional)

Instructions:

1. **Prepare the Cutlets:** Place each veal or pork cutlet between two sheets of plastic wrap or parchment paper. Using a meat mallet or the flat side of a heavy pan, gently pound the cutlets to an even thickness of about 1/4 inch. Season both sides of each cutlet with salt and freshly ground black pepper.

2. **Set Up a Dredging Station:** In three separate shallow dishes, set up a dredging station. Place the flour in the first dish, beat the eggs in the second dish, and spread the breadcrumbs in the third dish.

3. **Dredge the Cutlets:** One at a time, coat each cutlet in the flour, shaking off any excess. Next, dip it into the beaten eggs, allowing any excess to drip off. Finally, press it firmly into the breadcrumbs, ensuring that it's evenly coated on both sides. Set the breaded cutlets aside on a plate.

4. **Heat the Oil:** In a large skillet, heat enough vegetable oil to cover the bottom of the pan over medium-high heat. You'll need about 1/4 inch of oil. To test if the oil is hot enough, drop a small breadcrumb into the oil; it should sizzle and turn golden brown.

5. **Fry the Cutlets:** Carefully place the breaded cutlets in the hot oil, working in batches if necessary to avoid overcrowding the pan. Fry for about 2-3 minutes on each side, or until they turn golden brown and crispy. Use tongs to flip them gently.

Transfer the fried cutlets to a plate lined with paper towels to drain any excess oil.

6. **Serve:** Serve the Wiener Schnitzel hot, garnished with lemon wedges and, if desired, a sprig of parsley. The traditional way to enjoy it is with a squeeze of fresh lemon juice over the top.

7. **Enjoy:** Wiener Schnitzel is best enjoyed immediately while it's still hot and crispy.

Wiener Schnitzel is an Austrian classic that's loved around the world for its tender meat and golden, crispy breading. It's a timeless dish that's sure to please your taste buds.

Schweinsbraten (Roast Pork)

Schweinsbraten is a beloved Austrian dish consisting of succulent roast pork, often served with flavorful gravy and traditional sides like dumplings and sauerkraut. Here's how to make this delicious Austrian roast pork:

Ingredients:

For the Pork:

- 3-4 pounds (about 1.4-1.8 kg) boneless pork shoulder or pork loin roast
- 2 tablespoons vegetable oil
- Salt and freshly ground black pepper, to taste
- 2 cloves garlic, thinly sliced
- 1 small onion, sliced
- 1 tablespoon caraway seeds (optional, for a traditional flavor)
- 1-2 sprigs of fresh rosemary or thyme (or 1 teaspoon dried)

For the Gravy:

- 2 cups beef or vegetable broth
- 1/2 cup red wine (optional)
- 2 tablespoons all-purpose flour
- 2 tablespoons butter
- Salt and freshly ground black pepper, to taste

Instructions:

1. **Preheat the Oven:** Preheat your oven to 325°F (165°C).
2. **Prepare the Pork:** Pat the pork roast dry with paper towels. Season it generously with salt and freshly ground black pepper on all sides.
3. **Sear the Pork:** In a large ovenproof skillet or roasting pan, heat the vegetable oil over medium-high heat. Add the seasoned pork roast and sear it on all sides until it's well-browned. This step helps to develop flavor.

4. **Add Aromatics:** Remove the pork from the skillet and set it aside. In the same skillet, add the sliced garlic, onion, caraway seeds (if using), and fresh rosemary or thyme sprigs. Sauté for a few minutes until fragrant.

5. **Return the Pork:** Place the seared pork roast back into the skillet on top of the aromatic ingredients.

6. **Roast the Pork:** Transfer the skillet or roasting pan to the preheated oven. Roast the pork for about 2.5 to 3 hours, or until it reaches an internal temperature of 145°F (63°C) for slightly pink and juicy meat or 160°F (71°C) for fully cooked meat. Baste the pork occasionally with the pan juices during roasting.

7. **Rest the Pork:** Once the pork is done, remove it from the oven, tent it loosely with aluminum foil, and let it rest for about 15 minutes before slicing. This allows the juices to redistribute, resulting in tender and flavorful meat.

For the Gravy:

8. **Make the Gravy:** While the pork is resting, prepare the gravy. In a small saucepan, melt the butter over medium heat. Stir in the flour to create a roux, cooking it for about 2-3 minutes until it turns golden brown.

9. **Add Liquid:** Gradually whisk in the beef or vegetable broth and red wine (if using). Continue to whisk until the mixture thickens and comes to a simmer. Let it simmer for a few minutes until the gravy is smooth and flavorful. Season with salt and freshly ground black pepper to taste.

10. **Slice and Serve:** Slice the rested pork into thin slices and serve it with the delicious gravy. Traditionally, Schweinsbraten is served with dumplings,

sauerkraut, or potato salad, but you can choose your preferred sides.

11. **Enjoy:** Enjoy your homemade Schweinsbraten with all the traditional Austrian flavors and the tender, succulent pork.

Schweinsbraten is a quintessential Austrian dish that showcases the country's love for hearty, comforting meals. It's perfect for special occasions or a Sunday family dinner.

Rindsrouladen (Beef Roulades)

Rindsrouladen is a classic Austrian dish that consists of thinly sliced beef wrapped around a flavorful filling and simmered in a rich gravy. This dish is a true comfort food and a favorite in Austrian cuisine. Here's how to make it:

Ingredients:

For the Roulades:

- 4 slices of beef round or sirloin (about 1/4 inch thick and 4-6 inches wide)

- 4 slices of bacon
- 1 medium onion, finely chopped
- 2 dill pickles, sliced lengthwise
- 4 tablespoons mustard (Dijon or brown)
- Salt and freshly ground black pepper, to taste
- Toothpicks or kitchen twine, for securing

For the Gravy:

- 1 small onion, chopped
- 1 carrot, chopped
- 1 celery stalk, chopped
- 2 tablespoons vegetable oil
- 2 cups beef broth
- 1/2 cup red wine (optional)
- 2 tablespoons tomato paste
- 2 cloves garlic, minced
- 1 bay leaf
- 2 sprigs fresh thyme (or 1 teaspoon dried thyme)
- 2 tablespoons all-purpose flour
- Salt and freshly ground black pepper, to taste

Instructions:

For the Roulades:

1. **Prepare the Beef Slices:** Lay out the beef slices on a clean surface. Season each slice with salt and freshly ground black pepper.

2. **Layer the Fillings:** Spread about 1 tablespoon of mustard on each beef slice. Place a slice of bacon, some finely chopped onions, and a dill pickle slice on top of the mustard.

3. **Roll the Roulades:** Carefully roll up each beef slice with the fillings, securing them in place with toothpicks or kitchen twine.

4. **Sear the Roulades:** Heat the vegetable oil in a large skillet or Dutch oven over medium-high heat. Add the beef roulades and sear them on all sides until they are browned. Remove the roulades from the skillet and set them aside.

For the Gravy:

5. **Sauté Vegetables:** In the same skillet or Dutch oven, add the chopped onion, carrot, and celery. Sauté them until they become soft and lightly browned.

6. **Add Garlic and Tomato Paste:** Stir in the minced garlic and tomato paste, cooking for about a minute until fragrant.

7. **Deglaze the Pan:** Pour in the red wine (if using) and use a wooden spoon to scrape up any browned bits from the bottom of the skillet.

8. **Make the Gravy:** Sprinkle the all-purpose flour over the vegetables and stir well to combine. Gradually add the beef broth while continuing to stir, ensuring that there are no lumps. Add the bay leaf and thyme.

9. **Simmer the Roulades:** Return the seared beef roulades to the skillet with the gravy. Cover and let them simmer gently for about 1.5 to 2 hours, or until the beef is tender and the flavors meld together. Stir occasionally and add more beef broth or water if needed.

10. **Finish and Serve:** Once the roulades are done, remove them from the skillet and discard the toothpicks or twine. Season the gravy with salt and freshly ground black pepper to taste. If the gravy is too thin, you can thicken it with a bit of cornstarch or more flour mixed with water.

11. **Slice and Plate:** Slice the beef roulades into thick rounds and serve them with the rich gravy. Traditionally, Rindsrouladen is served with potato dumplings, spaetzle, or mashed potatoes, along with your choice of vegetables.

12. **Enjoy:** Enjoy your homemade Rindsrouladen, savoring the tender beef and flavorful filling with a generous serving of gravy.

Rindsrouladen is a comforting and savory Austrian dish that's perfect for special occasions or when you want to savor the flavors of traditional Austrian cuisine.

Tafelspitz (Boiled Beef with Horseradish)

Tafelspitz is a classic Austrian dish known for its simplicity and delicious flavors. It features slow-cooked beef served with a flavorful broth and accompanied by horseradish sauce and traditional side dishes. Here's how to make it:

Ingredients:

For the Beef:

- 2.5-3 pounds (about 1.1-1.4 kg) beef brisket or sirloin
- 1 onion, peeled and quartered
- 2 carrots, peeled and chopped
- 1 leek, cleaned and chopped
- 1 celery stalk, chopped
- 2 cloves garlic, smashed
- 2 bay leaves
- 8-10 whole peppercorns
- Salt, to taste
- Water

For the Horseradish Sauce:

- 1/2 cup prepared horseradish (or freshly grated horseradish)
- 1/2 cup sour cream
- 1 tablespoon white wine vinegar
- Salt and freshly ground black pepper, to taste

For Serving:

- Boiled potatoes, sliced into rounds
- Freshly grated horseradish (optional)
- Chopped fresh parsley (optional)

Instructions:

For the Beef:

1. **Prepare the Beef:** Place the beef brisket or sirloin in a large pot and add enough water to cover it. Bring the water to a boil, then reduce the heat to a gentle simmer.

2. **Add Vegetables and Spices:** Add the onion, carrots, leek, celery, garlic, bay leaves, whole peppercorns, and a pinch of salt to the pot.

3. **Simmer:** Let the beef simmer uncovered for about 2.5 to 3 hours, or until it becomes tender and easily pulls apart. Skim any impurities that rise to the surface during cooking.

4. **Strain and Reserve Broth:** Remove the beef from the broth and set it aside to cool. Strain the broth through a fine sieve or cheesecloth, reserving the flavorful broth for serving.

For the Horseradish Sauce:

5. **Prepare the Sauce:** In a bowl, combine the prepared horseradish (or freshly grated horseradish), sour cream, and white wine vinegar. Mix well. Season the sauce with salt and freshly ground black pepper to taste. Adjust the horseradish level to your preference, adding more for a stronger kick.

To Serve:

6. **Slice the Beef:** Once the beef has cooled, slice it thinly against the grain. The slices should be about 1/8 to 1/4 inch thick.

7. **Plate:** To serve, place slices of the boiled beef on plates alongside boiled potatoes.

8. **Add Broth:** Pour the hot, reserved broth over the beef and potatoes. The hot broth will help warm the beef and potatoes.

9. **Horseradish and Parsley:** Serve the Tafelspitz with the horseradish sauce on the side. If desired, garnish with freshly grated horseradish and chopped fresh parsley for additional flavor and freshness.

10. **Enjoy:** Enjoy your Tafelspitz, savoring the tender beef, flavorful broth, and zesty horseradish sauce.

Tafelspitz is a delightful Austrian dish that celebrates the art of slow-cooked beef. It's perfect for special occasions or when you want to experience the essence of traditional Austrian cuisine.

Kärntner Kasnudeln (Carinthian Cheese Noodles)

Kärntner Kasnudeln is a beloved dish from the Austrian region of Carinthia. It consists of tender pasta pockets filled with a savory cheese and potato mixture, often served with a simple brown butter sauce. Here's how to make this delicious Austrian specialty:

Ingredients:

For the Dough:

- 2 cups all-purpose flour
- 2 large eggs
- 1/2 cup water
- A pinch of salt

For the Filling:

- 2 large potatoes, peeled and diced
- 1 cup grated cheese (Carinthian varieties like Gailtaler Almkäse or Bergkäse are traditional, but you can use Swiss, Gruyère, or similar cheeses)
- 1 small onion, finely chopped
- 2 tablespoons butter
- Salt and freshly ground black pepper, to taste
- A pinch of nutmeg (optional)

For the Brown Butter Sauce:

- 1/2 cup unsalted butter
- Fresh sage leaves, for garnish (optional)
- Grated cheese, for garnish (optional)

Instructions:

For the Dough:

1. **Make the Dough:** In a mixing bowl, combine the flour and a pinch of salt. Make a well in the center and crack the eggs into it. Gradually add the water while mixing everything together until a smooth dough forms. Knead the dough for a few minutes

until it becomes elastic. Wrap it in plastic wrap and let it rest for about 30 minutes.

For the Filling:

2. **Prepare the Potatoes:** Boil the diced potatoes in salted water until they are tender. Drain and mash them while they are still warm.

3. **Sauté the Onion:** In a skillet, melt the butter over medium heat. Add the finely chopped onion and sauté until it becomes translucent and slightly golden.

4. **Mix Filling:** In a mixing bowl, combine the mashed potatoes, grated cheese, sautéed onion, and a pinch of nutmeg (if using). Season with salt and freshly ground black pepper to taste. Mix everything together to form the filling.

To Assemble:

5. **Roll Out the Dough:** On a lightly floured surface, roll out the dough into a thin sheet, about 1/8 inch thick.

6. **Cut Out Circles:** Using a round cookie cutter or a glass, cut out circles from the dough.

7. **Add Filling:** Place a small spoonful of the potato and cheese filling in the center of each dough circle. Fold the circles in half to create half-moon shapes, then pinch the edges together to seal the filling inside. You can also use a fork to crimp the edges for a decorative touch.

8. **Boil the Kasnudeln:** Bring a large pot of salted water to a boil. Add the Kasnudeln and cook them for about 3-4 minutes, or until they float to the surface. Remove them with a slotted spoon and set them aside.

For the Brown Butter Sauce:

9. **Brown the Butter:** In a saucepan, melt the unsalted butter over medium heat. Continue to cook it until it turns a golden brown color and emits a nutty aroma. Be careful not to burn it. You can add fresh sage leaves to the browned butter for extra flavor.

To Serve:

10. **Serve:** Place the boiled Kärntner Kasnudeln on plates and drizzle the brown butter sauce over them. If desired, garnish with grated cheese and fresh sage leaves.

11. **Enjoy:** Serve your Kärntner Kasnudeln hot, savoring the delightful combination of tender pasta pockets and the savory potato and cheese filling.

Kärntner Kasnudeln is a comforting and hearty Austrian dish that's sure to delight your taste buds with its rich flavors and traditional Alpine appeal.

Side Dishes
Erdäpfelsalat (Potato Salad)

Erdäpfelsalat is a popular Austrian potato salad that combines tender potatoes with a tangy and flavorful dressing. This salad is a staple at Austrian gatherings and pairs wonderfully with various main dishes, especially schnitzel. Here's how to make it:

Ingredients:

For the Potato Salad:

- 2 pounds (about 900g) waxy potatoes (such as Yukon Gold or red potatoes)
- 1 small red onion, finely chopped
- 3-4 cornichons or dill pickles, finely chopped
- 2 tablespoons fresh chives, finely chopped (optional)
- Salt and freshly ground black pepper, to taste

For the Dressing:

- 1/2 cup vegetable oil (such as sunflower or canola oil)
- 1/4 cup white wine vinegar or apple cider vinegar
- 1 tablespoon Dijon mustard
- 1-2 teaspoons granulated sugar, to taste
- Salt and freshly ground black pepper, to taste

Instructions:

1. **Boil the Potatoes:** Place the unpeeled potatoes in a large pot of cold, salted water. Bring the water to a boil and cook the potatoes until they are fork-tender, usually around 15-20 minutes, depending on their size. Be careful not to overcook them, as you want the potatoes to hold their shape.

2. **Cool and Peel:** Drain the potatoes and let them cool to room temperature. Once they are cool enough to handle, peel the potatoes and cut them into thin rounds, about 1/4 inch thick. Place the sliced potatoes in a large mixing bowl.

3. **Prepare the Dressing:** In a separate bowl, whisk together the vegetable oil, white wine vinegar or apple cider vinegar, Dijon mustard, and granulated sugar. Season the dressing with salt and freshly ground black pepper to taste. Taste the dressing and adjust the sugar, salt, or vinegar to achieve a balanced flavor.

4. **Combine Ingredients:** Add the finely chopped red onion, cornichons or dill pickles, and optional fresh chives to the sliced potatoes in the mixing bowl.

5. **Add the Dressing:** Pour the dressing over the potato mixture while the potatoes are still warm. Gently toss everything together to ensure that the potatoes are evenly coated with the dressing.

6. **Marinate:** Allow the potato salad to marinate for at least 30 minutes at room temperature. This allows the flavors to meld together and enhances the taste.

7. **Adjust Seasoning:** Before serving, taste the potato salad and adjust the seasoning with additional salt, pepper, or vinegar if needed.

8. **Serve:** Serve your Erdäpfelsalat at room temperature as a delightful side dish alongside Austrian favorites like schnitzel or bratwurst. It's also a great addition to picnics and barbecues.

9. **Enjoy:** Enjoy your homemade Erdäpfelsalat with its tangy and savory flavors that perfectly complement a wide range of dishes.

Erdäpfelsalat is a versatile and delicious Austrian potato salad that can be enjoyed year-round. Its simple yet flavorful ingredients make it a beloved side dish in Austrian cuisine.

Rotkraut (Red Cabbage)

Rotkraut, or red cabbage, is a popular side dish in Austrian cuisine known for its sweet and tangy flavor. It pairs wonderfully with hearty main courses like roasts and sausages. Here's how to make it:

Ingredients:

- 1 head of red cabbage
- 2 tablespoons vegetable oil or butter
- 1 medium onion, finely chopped
- 2-3 tart apples, peeled, cored, and chopped
- 2 cloves garlic, minced (optional)
- 1/2 cup red wine
- 1/4 cup red wine vinegar
- 2 tablespoons sugar (adjust to taste)
- 1/2 teaspoon ground cloves
- 1/2 teaspoon ground cinnamon
- Salt and freshly ground black pepper, to taste
- 1 bay leaf

Instructions:

1. **Prepare the Cabbage:** Remove the tough outer leaves of the red cabbage and discard them. Cut the cabbage into quarters and remove the core. Finely shred the cabbage using a sharp knife or a food processor.

2. **Sauté Onion and Garlic:** In a large, heavy-bottomed pot or Dutch oven, heat the vegetable oil or butter over medium heat. Add the finely chopped onion and minced garlic (if using). Sauté until the onion becomes translucent and fragrant.

3. **Add Cabbage:** Add the shredded red cabbage to the pot, stirring well to combine it with the sautéed onions. Cook for about 5-7 minutes, or until the cabbage begins to wilt.

4. **Add Apples:** Stir in the chopped tart apples, mixing them with the cabbage and onions.

5. **Deglaze with Red Wine:** Pour in the red wine to deglaze the pot, scraping up any browned bits from the bottom.

6. **Season and Simmer:** Add the red wine vinegar, sugar, ground cloves, ground cinnamon, salt, freshly ground black pepper, and the bay leaf. Stir everything together. Bring the mixture to a simmer.

7. **Simmer and Stir:** Reduce the heat to low and cover the pot. Let the Rotkraut simmer gently for about 45 minutes to 1 hour, or until the cabbage is tender and the flavors meld together. Stir occasionally, and add a splash of water if it starts to become too dry.

8. **Adjust Seasoning:** Taste the Rotkraut and adjust the seasoning with additional sugar, vinegar, salt, or spices if needed. The balance between sweet and tangy should suit your preference.

9. **Remove Bay Leaf:** Before serving, remove the bay leaf from the Rotkraut.

10. **Serve:** Serve your homemade Rotkraut hot as a delicious side dish alongside traditional Austrian mains like roasts, schnitzel, or sausages.

11. **Enjoy:** Enjoy the sweet and tangy flavors of Rotkraut as it complements your hearty Austrian meal.

Rotkraut is a versatile and flavorful side dish that adds a burst of color and taste to your Austrian culinary repertoire.

It's a perfect accompaniment to many traditional dishes and can be enjoyed year-round.

Knödel (Dumplings)

Dumplings, known as *Knödel* in Austria, are a versatile and beloved dish that can be served as a side dish or even as a main course. These hearty, doughy treats come in various forms and flavors, but one of the most classic Austrian versions is *Semmelknödel*, made from bread rolls. Here's how to make Semmelknödel:

Ingredients:

- 4-5 stale bread rolls or buns (preferably white or mixed wheat and rye)
- 1 cup milk
- 1 small onion, finely chopped
- 2-3 tablespoons butter
- 2 eggs

- Salt and freshly ground black pepper, to taste
- A pinch of ground nutmeg (optional)
- Chopped fresh parsley, for garnish (optional)

Instructions:

1. **Prepare the Bread:** Cut the stale bread rolls into small cubes or tear them into bite-sized pieces. Place the bread cubes in a large mixing bowl.

2. **Soak the Bread:** In a saucepan, heat the milk until it's warm but not boiling. Pour the warm milk over the bread cubes in the mixing bowl. Allow the bread to soak up the milk for about 15-20 minutes, or until it's softened and moistened.

3. **Sauté the Onion:** In a skillet, melt the butter over medium heat. Add the finely chopped onion and sauté until it becomes translucent and slightly golden. Remove the skillet from heat and let the onions cool.

4. **Mix the Dumpling Dough:** Once the bread is soaked and softened, add the sautéed onions, beaten eggs, salt, freshly ground black pepper, and ground nutmeg (if using) to the bread mixture. Mix everything together thoroughly until you have a sticky, uniform dough.

5. **Shape the Dumplings:** Wet your hands with cold water to prevent sticking. Take a portion of the dough and shape it into a round dumpling about the size of a tennis ball. Repeat with the remaining dough, placing each dumpling on a clean, floured surface or a parchment-lined tray.

6. **Boil the Dumplings:** In a large pot, bring salted water to a boil. Reduce the heat to a gentle simmer and carefully place the dumplings into the

simmering water. Let them cook for about 15-20 minutes, or until they float to the surface and are cooked through.

7. **Serve:** Using a slotted spoon, remove the dumplings from the water and drain them briefly on a clean kitchen towel or paper towels.

8. **Garnish:** If desired, garnish your Semmelknödel with chopped fresh parsley for color and a burst of freshness.

9. **Enjoy:** Serve your Knödel hot as a side dish to accompany a variety of Austrian dishes, such as sauerbraten, goulash, or roast meats.

Knödel come in many variations, including potato dumplings, spinach dumplings, and more. They are a comforting and filling addition to Austrian cuisine, loved for their ability to soak up rich gravies and sauces.

Semmelknödel (Bread Dumplings)

Semmelknödel are classic Austrian bread dumplings, often served as a side dish to complement hearty meat dishes and gravies. These dumplings are easy to make and incredibly delicious. Here's how to prepare them:

Ingredients:

- 6-8 stale bread rolls or buns (preferably white or mixed wheat and rye)
- 1 cup milk
- 1 small onion, finely chopped
- 2-3 tablespoons butter
- 2 eggs
- Salt and freshly ground black pepper, to taste
- A pinch of ground nutmeg (optional)
- Chopped fresh parsley, for garnish (optional)

Instructions:

1. **Prepare the Bread:** Cut the stale bread rolls into small cubes or tear them into bite-sized pieces. Place the bread cubes in a large mixing bowl.
2. **Soak the Bread:** In a saucepan, heat the milk until it's warm but not boiling. Pour the warm milk over the bread cubes in the mixing bowl. Allow the bread to soak up the milk for about 15-20 minutes, or until it's softened and moistened.
3. **Sauté the Onion:** In a skillet, melt the butter over medium heat. Add the finely chopped onion and sauté until it becomes translucent and slightly golden. Remove the skillet from heat and let the onions cool.

4. **Mix the Dumpling Dough:** Once the bread is soaked and softened, add the sautéed onions, beaten eggs, salt, freshly ground black pepper, and ground nutmeg (if using) to the bread mixture. Mix everything together thoroughly until you have a sticky, uniform dough.

5. **Shape the Dumplings:** Wet your hands with cold water to prevent sticking. Take a portion of the dough and shape it into a round dumpling about the size of a tennis ball. Repeat with the remaining dough, placing each dumpling on a clean, floured surface or a parchment-lined tray.

6. **Boil the Dumplings:** In a large pot, bring salted water to a boil. Reduce the heat to a gentle simmer and carefully place the dumplings into the simmering water. Let them cook for about 15-20 minutes, or until they float to the surface and are cooked through.

7. **Serve:** Using a slotted spoon, remove the dumplings from the water and drain them briefly on a clean kitchen towel or paper towels.

8. **Garnish:** If desired, garnish your Semmelknödel with chopped fresh parsley for color and a burst of freshness.

9. **Enjoy:** Serve your Semmelknödel hot as a side dish to accompany a variety of Austrian dishes, such as sauerbraten, goulash, or roast meats.

Semmelknödel are a delightful addition to Austrian cuisine, known for their comforting and hearty texture. They soak up gravies and sauces beautifully, making them a perfect pairing with rich meat dishes.

Sauerkraut

Sauerkraut is a traditional fermented cabbage dish that is widely enjoyed in Austrian cuisine, especially as a side dish to complement various main courses. It's made by fermenting finely shredded cabbage with salt, resulting in a tangy and flavorful condiment. Here's how to make sauerkraut:

Ingredients:

- 1 medium-sized green cabbage (about 2-3 pounds or 900g-1.4kg)
- 2 tablespoons kosher or pickling salt (avoid iodized salt)
- Caraway seeds or juniper berries (optional, for flavor)
- A large, clean glass or ceramic fermentation crock or a large glass jar with a lid

Instructions:

1. **Prepare the Cabbage:** Remove the outer leaves of the cabbage and set them aside. Core the

cabbage and shred it finely using a sharp knife, mandoline slicer, or a food processor.

2. **Salt and Massage:** In a large mixing bowl, combine the shredded cabbage and kosher or pickling salt. Massage the salt into the cabbage with clean hands, squeezing and kneading it for about 10 minutes. This helps the cabbage release its juices.

3. **Pack into a Container:** Begin filling your fermentation crock or glass jar with the salted cabbage. Pack the cabbage down tightly as you add it, making sure there are no air pockets. If you like, you can sprinkle some caraway seeds or juniper berries between the layers for added flavor.

4. **Use Cabbage Leaves:** Place the reserved cabbage leaves over the top of the packed cabbage. These leaves act as a barrier to keep the shredded cabbage submerged under its own juices.

5. **Weight It Down:** To ensure the cabbage remains submerged, place a clean, food-safe weight (a clean stone or a plastic bag filled with brine) on top of the cabbage leaves.

6. **Cover and Wait:** Cover the fermentation crock or jar with a clean cloth or plastic wrap secured with a rubber band or string. Allow the sauerkraut to ferment at room temperature for about 3-6 weeks, depending on the desired level of fermentation. Taste it occasionally to gauge the flavor.

7. **Check for Mold:** During fermentation, some white mold may develop on the surface. Skim it off and discard it. The sauerkraut beneath should be fine.

8. **Taste and Store:** Once the sauerkraut reaches the desired level of tanginess and fermentation, remove the weight, cabbage leaves, and any

excess surface mold. Transfer the sauerkraut to clean, airtight containers and store it in the refrigerator for several months.

9. **Serve:** Serve your homemade sauerkraut as a side dish alongside Austrian classics like sausages, schnitzel, or roast meats. It's also delicious in sandwiches and as a condiment.

10. **Enjoy:** Enjoy the tangy and probiotic-rich goodness of your homemade sauerkraut.

Sauerkraut is not only a tasty and versatile condiment but also a great source of probiotics and vitamins. It's a staple in Austrian cuisine and adds a delightful sour note to various dishes.

Vegetarian and Vegan Options
Gemüsestrudel (Vegetable Strudel)

Gemüsestrudel is a delightful Austrian pastry dish filled with a savory mixture of vegetables and herbs. It's a flavorful and comforting dish that's perfect for brunch, lunch, or dinner. Here's how to make it:

Ingredients:

For the Strudel Dough:

- 2 cups all-purpose flour
- 1/2 teaspoon salt
- 1/2 cup lukewarm water
- 2 tablespoons vegetable oil
- 1 egg, beaten (for brushing)

For the Vegetable Filling:

- 2 tablespoons butter
- 1 small onion, finely chopped
- 2 cloves garlic, minced
- 2 cups mixed vegetables (e.g., bell peppers, zucchini, carrots), diced
- 1 cup mushrooms, sliced
- 1 cup fresh spinach or Swiss chard, chopped
- 1/2 cup grated cheese (such as Gruyère or Swiss)
- 2 tablespoons fresh herbs (e.g., parsley, dill, chives), chopped
- Salt and freshly ground black pepper, to taste
- 1/4 teaspoon nutmeg (optional)
- 1/4 cup breadcrumbs (for the filling)

Instructions:

For the Strudel Dough:

1. **Prepare the Dough:** In a mixing bowl, combine the flour and salt. Gradually add the lukewarm water and vegetable oil while mixing until a dough forms. Knead the dough on a floured surface for about 5-10 minutes until it's smooth and elastic. Form it into a ball, coat it with a bit of oil, cover with a clean cloth, and let it rest for about 30 minutes.

For the Vegetable Filling:

2. **Sauté Onion and Garlic:** In a large skillet, melt the butter over medium heat. Add the finely chopped onion and minced garlic. Sauté until they become translucent.

3. **Add Vegetables:** Add the diced mixed vegetables, sliced mushrooms, and chopped spinach or Swiss chard to the skillet. Sauté for about 5-7 minutes, or until the vegetables are tender and any excess moisture has evaporated.

4. **Season and Add Herbs:** Season the vegetable mixture with salt, freshly ground black pepper, and nutmeg (if using). Stir in the chopped fresh herbs and grated cheese. Remove the skillet from heat and let the mixture cool slightly.

To Assemble:

5. **Preheat the Oven:** Preheat your oven to 375°F (190°C).

6. **Roll Out the Dough:** Roll out the rested strudel dough on a clean, floured surface into a large rectangle, about 12x16 inches (30x40 cm) or until it's thin and almost translucent. It should be thin enough to read a newspaper through.

7. **Add Filling:** Sprinkle the breadcrumbs evenly over the rolled-out dough to absorb any excess moisture from the filling. Then, spread the vegetable filling

evenly over the dough, leaving a small border along the edges.

8. **Roll and Seal:** Carefully lift one edge of the dough and start rolling it up, tucking in the sides as you go. Place the seam side down on a baking sheet lined with parchment paper. Tuck in the ends to seal the strudel.

9. **Brush with Egg:** Brush the beaten egg over the top of the strudel. This will give it a beautiful golden-brown color when baked.

10. **Bake:** Place the baking sheet in the preheated oven and bake for about 25-30 minutes, or until the strudel is crisp and golden.

11. **Cool and Slice:** Remove the Gemüsestrudel from the oven and let it cool for a few minutes before slicing it into portions.

12. **Serve:** Serve your Vegetable Strudel warm as a delightful and savory Austrian dish.

Gemüsestrudel is a flavorful and satisfying dish that showcases the deliciousness of fresh vegetables wrapped in flaky pastry. It's a fantastic addition to any Austrian meal or as a standalone dish for vegetarians and veggie lovers.

Eierschwammerlgulasch (Chanterelle Mushroom Goulash)

Eierschwammerlgulasch, also known as Chanterelle Mushroom Goulash, is a delicious and earthy Austrian dish that highlights the delicate flavor of chanterelle mushrooms. This vegetarian goulash is perfect for mushroom enthusiasts and those looking for a meat-free option. Here's how to make it:

Ingredients:

- 1 pound (450g) fresh chanterelle mushrooms, cleaned and halved or quartered if large
- 2 large onions, finely chopped
- 2 cloves garlic, minced
- 2 tablespoons vegetable oil
- 2 tablespoons tomato paste
- 2 tablespoons sweet paprika
- 1/2 teaspoon hot paprika (adjust to taste for spiciness)

- 1 red bell pepper, diced
- 1 yellow bell pepper, diced
- 1 green bell pepper, diced
- 2 large tomatoes, diced
- 2 bay leaves
- 1 teaspoon caraway seeds
- 1 cup vegetable broth
- 1 cup sour cream
- Salt and freshly ground black pepper, to taste
- Chopped fresh parsley, for garnish
- Cooked rice or spaetzle, for serving

Instructions:

1. **Sauté the Onions and Garlic:** In a large, heavy-bottomed pot, heat the vegetable oil over medium heat. Add the finely chopped onions and minced garlic. Sauté until the onions become translucent and fragrant.

2. **Add Tomato Paste and Paprika:** Stir in the tomato paste and both sweet and hot paprika. Cook for a couple of minutes to toast the spices, giving the goulash its rich color and flavor.

3. **Add Mushrooms:** Add the cleaned and halved or quartered chanterelle mushrooms to the pot. Sauté them with the onion mixture for about 5-7 minutes, allowing them to release their moisture and cook down.

4. **Incorporate Bell Peppers:** Add the diced red, yellow, and green bell peppers to the pot. Continue

to cook for another 5 minutes, allowing the peppers to soften.

5. **Add Tomatoes and Seasonings:** Stir in the diced tomatoes, bay leaves, and caraway seeds. Season with salt and freshly ground black pepper to taste.

6. **Simmer with Broth:** Pour in the vegetable broth and bring the goulash to a simmer. Let it cook for about 15-20 minutes, or until the mushrooms and peppers are tender, and the flavors meld together.

7. **Finish with Sour Cream:** Reduce the heat to low, and then gently stir in the sour cream. Simmer for an additional 5-7 minutes, allowing the flavors to meld and the goulash to thicken slightly. Adjust the seasoning if needed.

8. **Garnish and Serve:** Remove the bay leaves from the goulash. Garnish with chopped fresh parsley for a burst of color and freshness.

9. **Serve:** Serve your Eierschwammerlgulasch hot over cooked rice or spaetzle, which pairs wonderfully with the creamy and flavorful mushroom goulash.

10. **Enjoy:** Savor the delicious and hearty flavors of this Austrian Chanterelle Mushroom Goulash, perfect for a comforting and satisfying meal.

Eierschwammerlgulasch is a delightful Austrian dish that celebrates the unique and delicate taste of chanterelle mushrooms. It's a warm and flavorful option for both vegetarians and mushroom lovers alike.

Krautfleckerl (Cabbage Pasta)

Krautfleckerl is a traditional Austrian dish that combines pasta with sautéed cabbage and onions, resulting in a comforting and hearty meal. It's a simple yet flavorful recipe that's perfect for those seeking a taste of Austrian home cooking. Here's how to make it:

Ingredients:

- 8 ounces (about 225g) pasta (typically egg noodles or wide flat noodles)
- 1 small head of green cabbage, shredded
- 1 large onion, finely chopped
- 3 tablespoons vegetable oil
- 1 teaspoon caraway seeds (optional)
- 2 cloves garlic, minced (optional)
- Salt and freshly ground black pepper, to taste
- Chopped fresh parsley, for garnish (optional)

Instructions:

1. **Cook the Pasta:** Bring a large pot of salted water to a boil. Cook the pasta according to the package instructions until al dente. Drain and set aside.
2. **Sauté the Onions:** In a large skillet or frying pan, heat the vegetable oil over medium heat. Add the finely chopped onion and sauté until it becomes translucent and slightly golden.
3. **Add Cabbage and Seasonings:** Add the shredded cabbage to the skillet, along with the caraway seeds (if using) and minced garlic (if desired). Sauté the cabbage, stirring occasionally, until it wilts and becomes tender. This should take about 10-15 minutes.
4. **Combine Pasta and Cabbage:** Once the cabbage is tender, add the cooked pasta to the skillet. Toss everything together to combine the pasta and cabbage evenly. Continue to cook for a few minutes, allowing the flavors to meld together.
5. **Season and Garnish:** Season the Krautfleckerl with salt and freshly ground black pepper to taste. If desired, garnish with chopped fresh parsley for a burst of color and freshness.
6. **Serve:** Serve your Krautfleckerl hot as a comforting and hearty Austrian dish.

Krautfleckerl is a straightforward yet delicious Austrian recipe that showcases the wonderful combination of pasta and cabbage. It's a comforting and satisfying meal, perfect for a taste of traditional Austrian home cooking.

Spinatknödel (Spinach Dumplings)

Spinatknödel are delightful Austrian dumplings made with spinach and bread. These dumplings are both hearty and comforting, making them a wonderful addition to your Austrian cuisine repertoire. Here's how to make them:

Ingredients:

For the Dumplings:

- 8 ounces (about 225g) fresh spinach
- 4 cups stale bread cubes (such as white or whole wheat bread)
- 1/2 cup milk
- 2 tablespoons butter
- 1 small onion, finely chopped
- 2 cloves garlic, minced (optional)
- 2 eggs
- 1/4 cup grated Parmesan cheese

- Salt and freshly ground black pepper, to taste
- A pinch of ground nutmeg (optional)
- 2-3 tablespoons all-purpose flour (for dusting)

For the Brown Butter Sauce:

- 1/2 cup unsalted butter
- Fresh sage leaves (optional, for garnish)
- Grated Parmesan cheese (optional, for garnish)

Instructions:

For the Dumplings:

1. **Prepare the Spinach:** Rinse the fresh spinach thoroughly and remove any tough stems. Bring a pot of water to a boil and blanch the spinach for about 1-2 minutes until wilted. Drain and rinse the spinach with cold water to stop the cooking process. Squeeze out excess water and finely chop the spinach.

2. **Soak the Bread:** In a bowl, soak the stale bread cubes in milk until they are soft and mushy. Squeeze out any excess milk.

3. **Sauté Onion and Garlic:** In a skillet, melt the butter over medium heat. Add the finely chopped onion and minced garlic (if using). Sauté until the onion becomes translucent and slightly golden.

4. **Mix the Dumpling Batter:** In a large mixing bowl, combine the soaked bread cubes, sautéed onions and garlic, chopped spinach, eggs, grated Parmesan cheese, salt, freshly ground black pepper, and a pinch of ground nutmeg (if using). Mix everything together until you have a sticky dough. If the dough is too wet, you can add a bit more flour to adjust the consistency.

5. **Form the Dumplings:** Wet your hands with cold water to prevent sticking. Take portions of the dough and shape them into round dumplings, about the size of a tennis ball. Roll each dumpling in a bit of flour to coat lightly.
6. **Boil the Dumplings:** Bring a large pot of salted water to a boil. Carefully place the dumplings into the boiling water. Let them cook for about 15-20 minutes, or until they float to the surface and are cooked through.

For the Brown Butter Sauce:

7. **Brown the Butter:** While the dumplings are cooking, prepare the brown butter sauce. In a saucepan, melt the unsalted butter over medium heat. Continue to cook it until it turns a golden brown color and emits a nutty aroma. Be careful not to burn it. You can add fresh sage leaves to the browned butter for extra flavor.
8. **Serve:** Place the boiled Spinatknödel on plates and drizzle the brown butter sauce over them. If desired, garnish with grated Parmesan cheese and fresh sage leaves.
9. **Enjoy:** Serve your Spinatknödel hot, savoring the delightful combination of tender spinach dumplings and the rich brown butter sauce.

Spinatknödel are a comforting and flavorful Austrian dish that's perfect for both vegetarians and those looking for a hearty and satisfying meal.

Kürbiscremesuppe (Pumpkin Cream Soup)

Kürbiscremesuppe, or Pumpkin Cream Soup, is a warm and comforting Austrian soup that's especially popular during the autumn season when pumpkins are in abundance. This creamy and flavorful soup is perfect as an appetizer or a light main course. Here's how to make it:

Ingredients:

- 2 pounds (about 900g) pumpkin, peeled, seeded, and cubed
- 1 large onion, chopped
- 2 cloves garlic, minced
- 2 tablespoons butter
- 4 cups vegetable or chicken broth
- 1 cup heavy cream
- 1/2 teaspoon ground nutmeg
- Salt and freshly ground black pepper, to taste
- Chopped fresh parsley or chives, for garnish

- Pumpkin seeds, toasted (optional, for garnish)

Instructions:

1. **Prepare the Pumpkin:** Start by peeling and seeding the pumpkin, then cut it into cubes. You can use various types of pumpkin, but butternut squash is a good choice for its sweet flavor and smooth texture.

2. **Sauté Onion and Garlic:** In a large pot or Dutch oven, melt the butter over medium heat. Add the chopped onion and minced garlic. Sauté until the onion becomes translucent and fragrant.

3. **Add Pumpkin:** Add the cubed pumpkin to the pot and sauté with the onion and garlic for a few minutes, allowing the pumpkin to absorb some of the flavors.

4. **Add Broth:** Pour in the vegetable or chicken broth, ensuring that the pumpkin is fully covered. Bring the mixture to a boil, then reduce the heat to a simmer. Cover the pot and let it cook for about 20-25 minutes, or until the pumpkin is tender and easily pierced with a fork.

5. **Puree the Soup:** Using an immersion blender or a regular blender (in batches), carefully puree the soup until it's smooth and creamy.

6. **Season and Add Cream:** Return the pureed soup to the pot over low heat. Season it with ground nutmeg, salt, and freshly ground black pepper. Stir in the heavy cream, and let the soup simmer for an additional 5-10 minutes to heat through.

7. **Adjust Consistency:** If the soup is too thick, you can add a bit more broth or water to reach your desired consistency. If it's too thin, simmer it a bit longer to thicken.

8. **Serve:** Ladle the hot Kürbiscremesuppe into bowls. Garnish each serving with chopped fresh parsley or chives, and optionally, toasted pumpkin seeds for added texture and flavor.

9. **Enjoy:** Serve your Pumpkin Cream Soup hot, savoring its rich and velvety texture, complemented by the earthy sweetness of the pumpkin and the warm spices.

Kürbiscremesuppe is a delightful and comforting soup that's perfect for warming up on a chilly day or as an elegant starter for a special meal. Its smooth and creamy texture, combined with the flavors of pumpkin and nutmeg, make it a true Austrian favorite.

Desserts and Pastries
Apfelstrudel (Apple Strudel)

Apfelstrudel is a beloved Austrian pastry that's famous for its delicate layers of flaky pastry wrapped around a sweet and spiced apple filling. It's a classic dessert that's enjoyed in Austria and beyond. Here's how to make it:

Ingredients:

For the Strudel Dough:

- 2 cups all-purpose flour
- 1/4 teaspoon salt
- 1/2 cup lukewarm water
- 2 tablespoons vegetable oil
- 1 egg, beaten (for brushing)

For the Apple Filling:

- 6-7 medium-sized apples (such as Granny Smith or Braeburn), peeled, cored, and thinly sliced
- 1 cup breadcrumbs
- 1/2 cup granulated sugar
- 1 teaspoon ground cinnamon
- 1/2 cup raisins (optional)
- 1/2 cup chopped walnuts (optional)
- Zest of 1 lemon
- Juice of 1 lemon
- 2 tablespoons melted butter

Instructions:

For the Strudel Dough:

1. **Prepare the Dough:** In a mixing bowl, combine the flour and salt. Gradually add the lukewarm water and vegetable oil while mixing until a dough forms. Knead the dough on a floured surface for about 10-

15 minutes until it's smooth and elastic. Form it into a ball, coat it with a bit of oil, cover with a clean cloth, and let it rest for about 30 minutes.

For the Apple Filling:

2. **Prepare the Apples:** Peel, core, and thinly slice the apples. Toss them in a bowl with lemon juice and lemon zest to prevent browning.

3. **Make the Filling Mixture:** In a separate bowl, combine the breadcrumbs, granulated sugar, ground cinnamon, raisins (if using), and chopped walnuts (if using). Mix well.

To Assemble:

4. **Roll Out the Dough:** Roll out the rested strudel dough on a clean, floured surface into a large rectangle, about 12x16 inches (30x40 cm) or until it's thin enough to read a newspaper through. It should be paper-thin.

5. **Add the Apple Filling:** Sprinkle the breadcrumb mixture evenly over the rolled-out dough. Arrange the sliced apples on top of the breadcrumb mixture.

6. **Roll and Tuck:** Carefully lift one edge of the dough and start rolling it up, tucking in the sides as you go. Place the seam side down on a baking sheet lined with parchment paper. Tuck in the ends to seal the strudel.

7. **Brush with Egg:** Brush the beaten egg over the top of the strudel. This will give it a beautiful golden-brown color when baked.

8. **Bake:** Preheat your oven to 375°F (190°C). Place the baking sheet in the preheated oven and bake for

about 30-35 minutes, or until the Apfelstrudel is crisp and golden.

9. **Cool and Slice:** Remove the Apfelstrudel from the oven and let it cool for a few minutes before slicing it into portions.

10. **Serve:** Serve your Apple Strudel warm, dusted with powdered sugar if desired. It's also delicious with a scoop of vanilla ice cream or a dollop of whipped cream.

11. **Enjoy:** Savor the sweet and spiced apple filling wrapped in flaky layers of pastry in this classic Austrian dessert.

Apfelstrudel is a delightful dessert that's known for its beautiful layers and the comforting aroma of baked apples and spices. It's a beloved Austrian pastry that's perfect for any occasion.

Sachertorte (Sacher Torte)

Sachertorte is a famous Austrian chocolate cake known for its rich, dense chocolate layers and a layer of apricot jam. It's traditionally served with a glossy chocolate glaze on top. This exquisite dessert is a true Austrian classic and a must-try for chocolate lovers. Here's how to make it:

Ingredients:

For the Cake:

- 4 ounces (115g) bittersweet chocolate, finely chopped
- 1/2 cup (1 stick or 113g) unsalted butter, softened
- 3/4 cup (150g) granulated sugar
- 6 large eggs, separated
- 1 teaspoon vanilla extract
- 1 cup (120g) all-purpose flour
- 1/4 cup (25g) unsweetened cocoa powder
- 1/2 teaspoon salt

For the Filling:

- 1/2 cup apricot jam or preserves

For the Chocolate Glaze:

- 4 ounces (115g) bittersweet chocolate, finely chopped
- 1/2 cup (120ml) heavy cream
- 2 tablespoons unsalted butter
- 2 tablespoons powdered sugar
- 1/4 cup (30g) unsweetened cocoa powder

Instructions:

For the Cake:

1. **Preheat the Oven:** Preheat your oven to 350°F (175°C). Grease a 9-inch (23 cm) round cake pan and line the bottom with parchment paper.

2. **Melt Chocolate:** In a heatproof bowl set over simmering water (or in the microwave), melt the finely chopped bittersweet chocolate until smooth. Set it aside to cool slightly.

3. **Cream Butter and Sugar:** In a large mixing bowl, beat the softened butter and granulated sugar together until light and fluffy.

4. **Add Egg Yolks and Vanilla:** Add the egg yolks one at a time, beating well after each addition. Mix in the vanilla extract.

5. **Incorporate Chocolate:** Gradually add the melted chocolate to the butter mixture and mix until well combined.

6. **Sift Dry Ingredients:** In a separate bowl, sift together the all-purpose flour, unsweetened cocoa powder, and salt.

7. **Combine Wet and Dry Mixtures:** Gently fold the dry ingredients into the chocolate mixture until just combined. Be careful not to overmix.

8. **Whip Egg Whites:** In a clean, dry bowl, whip the egg whites until stiff peaks form.

9. **Fold in Egg Whites:** Carefully fold the whipped egg whites into the cake batter in two or three additions, using a gentle folding motion to maintain the cake's lightness.

10. **Bake:** Pour the batter into the prepared cake pan and smooth the top. Bake in the preheated oven

for about 35-40 minutes, or until a toothpick inserted into the center comes out clean.

11. **Cool:** Allow the cake to cool in the pan for about 10 minutes, then remove it from the pan and let it cool completely on a wire rack.

Assemble the Sachertorte:

12. **Cut and Fill:** Once the cake has cooled, carefully slice it horizontally into two even layers. Spread the apricot jam evenly over the bottom layer, then place the second layer on top.

For the Chocolate Glaze:

13. **Prepare Chocolate Glaze:** In a small saucepan, heat the heavy cream and butter until it begins to simmer. Remove from heat and add the finely chopped bittersweet chocolate. Let it sit for a minute, then stir until the chocolate is fully melted and the mixture is smooth. Sift in the powdered sugar and cocoa powder, stirring until well combined.

14. **Glaze the Cake:** Pour the warm chocolate glaze evenly over the top and sides of the cake. Use a spatula to smooth the glaze, creating a glossy finish.

15. **Set and Serve:** Allow the glaze to set for a few hours at room temperature or in the refrigerator. Slice and serve your Sachertorte, traditionally with a dollop of whipped cream.

Enjoy the decadent layers of chocolate and apricot in this iconic Austrian dessert!

Linzer Torte (Linzer Cake)

Linzer Torte is a classic Austrian pastry known for its crumbly and buttery almond-based crust filled with a layer of fruity jam, often raspberry or black currant, and topped with a lattice crust. It's a delightful treat with a beautiful presentation. Here's how to make it:

Ingredients:

For the Crust:

- 1 1/2 cups (180g) all-purpose flour
- 1 1/2 cups (150g) ground almonds or almond flour
- 1/2 cup (100g) granulated sugar
- 1 teaspoon ground cinnamon
- 1/2 teaspoon ground cloves
- 1/2 teaspoon lemon zest
- 1/2 cup (1 stick or 113g) unsalted butter, cold and cubed
- 1 large egg

For the Filling:

- 1 1/2 cups raspberry or black currant jam

For the Topping:

- Powdered sugar, for dusting

Instructions:

1. **Prepare the Crust:** In a large mixing bowl, combine the all-purpose flour, ground almonds or almond flour, granulated sugar, ground cinnamon, ground cloves, and lemon zest.

2. **Cut in Butter:** Add the cold, cubed unsalted butter to the dry ingredients. Use a pastry cutter or your fingers to work the butter into the dry ingredients until the mixture resembles coarse crumbs.

3. **Add Egg:** Beat the large egg in a separate bowl and then add it to the mixture. Stir until the dough comes together. If it seems too dry, you can add a teaspoon of cold water at a time until it reaches the right consistency.

4. **Chill the Dough:** Shape the dough into a disk, wrap it in plastic wrap, and refrigerate for about 1 hour or until it's firm.

5. **Preheat the Oven:** Preheat your oven to 350°F (175°C). Grease a 9-inch (23 cm) tart or springform pan.

6. **Roll Out the Dough:** On a lightly floured surface, roll out about two-thirds of the dough into a circle large enough to fit the bottom and sides of the prepared pan. Transfer the dough to the pan, pressing it gently to fit.

7. **Spread the Jam:** Spread the raspberry or black currant jam evenly over the bottom crust.

8. **Create the Lattice:** Roll out the remaining dough and cut it into thin strips. Create a lattice pattern on top of the jam by arranging the strips in a crisscross pattern. Trim any excess dough hanging over the edges.

9. **Bake:** Place the Linzer Torte in the preheated oven and bake for about 30-35 minutes, or until the crust is golden brown.

10. **Cool:** Allow the Linzer Torte to cool completely in the pan on a wire rack.

11. **Dust with Powdered Sugar:** Before serving, dust the top of the Linzer Torte with powdered sugar for a decorative finish.

12. **Serve:** Slice and serve your Linzer Torte as a delightful Austrian dessert, perfect for afternoon tea or any special occasion.

This Linzer Torte is a delicious and elegant treat that combines the flavors of almonds and fruity jam in a beautifully crafted dessert. Enjoy its rich and crumbly texture!

Topfenstrudel (Quark Strudel)

Topfenstrudel is a delightful Austrian pastry that features a flaky, buttery pastry wrapped around a sweet and creamy quark (curd cheese) filling. It's a beloved dessert in Austria and is often enjoyed with a dusting of powdered sugar or a dollop of whipped cream. Here's how to make it:

Ingredients:

For the Strudel Dough:

- 2 cups all-purpose flour
- 1/4 teaspoon salt
- 1/2 cup lukewarm water
- 2 tablespoons vegetable oil
- 1 egg, beaten (for brushing)

For the Quark Filling:

- 2 cups quark (curd cheese)
- 1/2 cup granulated sugar

- 2 large eggs
- 1 teaspoon vanilla extract
- 1/2 teaspoon lemon zest (optional)
- 1/4 cup raisins (optional)
- 2 tablespoons unsalted butter, melted

Instructions:

For the Strudel Dough:

1. **Prepare the Dough:** In a mixing bowl, combine the flour and salt. Gradually add the lukewarm water and vegetable oil while mixing until a dough forms. Knead the dough on a floured surface for about 10-15 minutes until it's smooth and elastic. Form it into a ball, coat it with a bit of oil, cover with a clean cloth, and let it rest for about 30 minutes.

For the Quark Filling:

2. **Prepare the Quark Mixture:** In a separate mixing bowl, combine the quark, granulated sugar, eggs, vanilla extract, and lemon zest (if using). Mix until the filling is smooth and well combined. If desired, stir in the raisins.

To Assemble:

3. **Roll Out the Dough:** Roll out the rested strudel dough on a clean, floured surface into a large rectangle, about 12x16 inches (30x40 cm) or until it's thin enough to read a newspaper through. It should be very thin.

4. **Add the Quark Filling:** Spread the quark mixture evenly over the rolled-out dough, leaving a small border along the edges.

5. **Fold and Roll:** Carefully lift one edge of the dough and start rolling it up, tucking in the sides as you go. Place the seam side down on a baking sheet lined with parchment paper.

6. **Brush with Egg:** Brush the beaten egg over the top of the strudel. This will give it a beautiful golden-brown color when baked.

7. **Bake:** Preheat your oven to 375°F (190°C). Place the baking sheet in the preheated oven and bake for about 30-35 minutes, or until the Topfenstrudel is crisp and golden.

8. **Cool and Slice:** Remove the Topfenstrudel from the oven and let it cool for a few minutes before slicing it into portions.

9. **Serve:** Serve your Quark Strudel warm, dusted with powdered sugar or accompanied by a dollop of whipped cream.

10. **Enjoy:** Savor the sweet and creamy quark filling wrapped in flaky layers of pastry in this classic Austrian dessert.

Topfenstrudel is a delightful and comforting Austrian dessert that showcases the creamy goodness of quark cheese in a beautifully crafted pastry. It's a treat that's sure to please your taste buds.

Mozartkugeln (Mozart Balls)

Mozartkugeln are a famous Austrian confection named after the renowned composer Wolfgang Amadeus Mozart. These delightful sweets are made of marzipan, nougat, and dark chocolate, creating a harmonious blend of flavors and textures. Here's how to make them:

Ingredients:

For the Marzipan Filling:

- 7 ounces (200g) marzipan
- 2 teaspoons pistachio paste (optional, for color)
- 1 teaspoon rosewater (optional, for flavor)

For the Nougat Filling:

- 3.5 ounces (100g) nougat (typically hazelnut nougat)

For the Chocolate Coating:

- 8 ounces (225g) dark chocolate, melted

For Decoration:

- 1.5 ounces (45g) pistachios, finely chopped
- 1.5 ounces (45g) powdered sugar

Instructions:

For the Marzipan Filling:

1. **Prepare Marzipan:** In a mixing bowl, crumble the marzipan and knead it until it's soft and pliable. If you're using pistachio paste and rosewater, add them to the marzipan and knead until well combined. This step is optional but adds color and flavor to the marzipan.

For the Nougat Filling:

2. **Shape Nougat Balls:** Divide the nougat into small pieces and shape them into small balls, roughly the size of a hazelnut.

Assemble the Mozartkugeln:

3. **Wrap in Marzipan:** Take a small portion of the marzipan and flatten it in the palm of your hand. Place a nougat ball in the center and wrap the marzipan around it, shaping it into a ball. Ensure the nougat is completely covered by the marzipan. Repeat this step for all the nougat pieces.

4. **Coat with Chocolate:** Melt the dark chocolate using a double boiler or microwave, and let it cool slightly. Using a fork or a chocolate dipping tool, dip each marzipan-nougat ball into the melted chocolate, ensuring it's fully coated. Allow any excess chocolate to drip off, and then place the coated balls on a parchment-lined tray.

5. **Decorate:** While the chocolate is still slightly soft, sprinkle the finely chopped pistachios over the top of each Mozartkugel.

6. **Chill:** Place the tray in the refrigerator for about 30 minutes to allow the chocolate to set.

7. **Dust with Powdered Sugar:** Once the chocolate is completely set, dust the Mozartkugeln with powdered sugar. This step adds a decorative touch and helps recreate the appearance of Mozart's powdered wigs.

8. **Serve:** Arrange your homemade Mozart Balls on a plate or in a box for a delightful and decadent treat.

9. **Enjoy:** Savor the harmonious blend of marzipan, nougat, and dark chocolate in each Mozartkugel. These sweet confections pay homage to the musical genius Wolfgang Amadeus Mozart and are a beloved Austrian delicacy.

Mozartkugeln are a delightful treat that combines different textures and flavors to create a memorable confection. Enjoy these sweet creations as a special treat or gift them to friends and loved ones.

Beverages
Glühwein (Mulled Wine)

Glühwein is a warm and aromatic beverage that's especially popular during the winter months, particularly around Christmas markets in Austria and Germany. This spiced mulled wine is perfect for warming up on a cold day and is enjoyed by many as a festive holiday drink. Here's how to make it:

Ingredients:

- 1 bottle (750 ml) of red wine (choose a robust red wine like Merlot or Cabernet Sauvignon)
- 1/4 cup (50g) granulated sugar (adjust to taste)
- 1 orange, thinly sliced
- 1 lemon, thinly sliced
- 10 whole cloves
- 2-3 cinnamon sticks
- 3-4 star anise pods

- 5-6 cardamom pods (lightly crushed)
- 1 vanilla bean, split lengthwise (optional)
- Orange peel strips, for garnish (optional)

Instructions:

1. **Prepare the Ingredients:** Thinly slice the orange and lemon. If using a vanilla bean, split it lengthwise to expose the seeds.

2. **Combine Ingredients:** In a large saucepan or pot, pour in the red wine and add the granulated sugar, orange slices, lemon slices, cloves, cinnamon sticks, star anise pods, cardamom pods, and the split vanilla bean (if using).

3. **Warm Gently:** Place the saucepan over low to medium-low heat. It's important not to boil the wine but to gently warm it. Stir occasionally to help dissolve the sugar. Allow the mixture to warm for about 20-30 minutes. You should start to smell the wonderful spiced aroma.

4. **Simmer (Optional):** If you have more time, you can let the mixture simmer for up to an hour to infuse the flavors even more. Keep it covered during this time to prevent too much evaporation.

5. **Strain and Serve:** Once the Glühwein has reached the desired level of spiced aroma and flavor, remove it from the heat. Use a fine-mesh strainer to strain out all the spices and fruit slices, transferring the mulled wine into a serving pot or individual mugs.

6. **Garnish (Optional):** If desired, garnish each mug with a strip of orange peel.

7. **Serve Hot:** Serve your homemade Glühwein while it's still hot, either in mugs or heatproof glasses. Enjoy

the warm, spiced goodness of this classic holiday beverage.

8. **Variations:** Feel free to adjust the sweetness to your liking by adding more or less sugar. You can also experiment with different spices or add a shot of rum, brandy, or amaretto for an extra kick.

9. **Enjoy Responsibly:** Remember to enjoy your Glühwein responsibly, especially if you choose to include alcohol.

Glühwein is a delightful and warming holiday drink that's perfect for festive gatherings, winter evenings by the fireplace, or a cozy night in. Its aromatic spices and fruity notes make it a cherished holiday tradition in many European countries.

Almdudler (Austrian Herbal Soda)

Almdudler is a beloved Austrian soft drink known for its unique herbal and fruity flavor. It's often enjoyed as a refreshing beverage, especially during the summer months or as a non-alcoholic alternative to beer in Austria. Here's how to make a homemade version of Almdudler:

Ingredients:

- 1 liter (about 4 cups) sparkling water or club soda
- 1/2 cup clear apple juice (or white grape juice as a substitute)
- 1/4 cup lemon juice (from about 2-3 lemons)
- 2 tablespoons honey or agave nectar (adjust to taste)
- 1 teaspoon dried lemon balm leaves (or fresh, if available)
- 1 teaspoon dried elderflower (or fresh, if available)
- 1/2 teaspoon dried marjoram leaves (or fresh, if available)
- 1/2 teaspoon dried gentian root (optional, for a bitter note)
- Ice cubes, lemon slices, and fresh herbs for garnish (optional)

Instructions:

1. **Prepare the Herbal Infusion:** In a small saucepan, combine the dried lemon balm leaves, dried elderflower, dried marjoram leaves, and dried gentian root (if using) with 1/2 cup of water. Bring the mixture to a gentle simmer, then remove it from the heat. Allow the herbs to steep for about 15-20 minutes, infusing the water with their flavors.

2. **Strain the Herbal Infusion:** After steeping, strain the herbal infusion through a fine-mesh sieve or cheesecloth to remove the solid herb particles. You should be left with a clear herbal liquid.

3. **Sweeten the Mixture:** While the herbal infusion is still warm, stir in the honey or agave nectar until it's completely dissolved. Adjust the sweetness to your liking.

4. **Cool Down:** Allow the herbal mixture to cool to room temperature. You can speed up the cooling process by placing it in the refrigerator.

5. **Mix the Soda:** In a large pitcher, combine the sparkling water or club soda, clear apple juice (or white grape juice), and lemon juice. Stir to mix.

6. **Add the Herbal Infusion:** Pour the cooled herbal infusion into the soda mixture and stir well.

7. **Chill:** Place the Almdudler in the refrigerator to chill for at least 30 minutes, allowing the flavors to meld.

8. **Serve:** When ready to serve, fill glasses with ice cubes and pour the homemade Almdudler over the ice. Garnish with lemon slices and fresh herbs if desired.

9. **Enjoy:** Sip and savor your homemade Almdudler, relishing its unique blend of herbal, fruity, and slightly tangy flavors.

Almdudler is a refreshing and unique Austrian soda that captures the essence of the Alpine region. Making it at home allows you to adjust the sweetness and herbal flavors to your preference, providing a delightful alternative to commercial soft drinks.

Wiener Melange (Viennese Coffee)

Wiener Melange is a classic Austrian coffee specialty that combines espresso with steamed milk and a dollop of frothy milk foam, similar to a cappuccino or a latte. It's a beloved coffee drink in Vienna and is often served with a small glass of water. Here's how to make it:

Ingredients:

- 1 shot of espresso (approximately 1 ounce or 30ml)
- 3/4 cup (180ml) hot, steamed milk
- A dollop of milk foam (about 2-3 tablespoons)
- Sugar, to taste (optional)
- Whipped cream and chocolate shavings for garnish (optional)

Instructions:

1. **Brew Espresso:** Start by brewing a shot of espresso using your espresso machine. If you don't have an espresso machine, you can use a stovetop espresso

maker or a strong cup of brewed coffee as a substitute.

2. **Steam Milk:** While the espresso is brewing, steam the milk using a milk frother or a steam wand on an espresso machine. The milk should be hot and have a velvety texture, with microfoam created during the steaming process.

3. **Pour Espresso:** Pour the freshly brewed espresso into a coffee mug or a glass.

4. **Add Steamed Milk:** Carefully pour the hot, steamed milk into the espresso, holding back the frothy milk foam with a spoon to let the milk flow first.

5. **Add Foam:** Top the coffee with a dollop of milk foam. You can scoop it out with a spoon or use a milk frother to create the foam.

6. **Sweeten (Optional):** If desired, sweeten your Wiener Melange with sugar to taste. Stir until the sugar is completely dissolved.

7. **Garnish (Optional):** For an extra touch of indulgence, garnish your Wiener Melange with a dollop of whipped cream and a sprinkle of chocolate shavings.

8. **Serve:** Serve your Wiener Melange immediately, traditionally accompanied by a small glass of water.

9. **Enjoy:** Sip and savor the rich, creamy, and aromatic flavors of your homemade Viennese coffee.

Wiener Melange is a delightful coffee beverage that's perfect for enjoying a moment of relaxation or as a treat during your morning routine. Its smooth and velvety texture, combined with the bold flavors of espresso, make it a favorite among coffee enthusiasts in Austria and beyond.

Sturm (Young Wine)

Sturm is a seasonal Austrian beverage that's celebrated in the wine-growing regions during the autumn harvest season. It's also known as "Federweißer" in Germany. Sturm is essentially young, partially fermented wine that is still in the early stages of fermentation. It's cloudy and sweet with a slight fizz and is typically enjoyed as a seasonal treat. Here's how Sturm is made and enjoyed:

Production:

1. **Harvest Grapes:** Sturm is made from freshly harvested grapes, often from varieties like Grüner Veltliner or Welschriesling. These grapes are picked at the peak of ripeness.

2. **Crush Grapes:** The grapes are crushed, and the juice is extracted. Unlike regular wine, Sturm is made without the addition of any additives or sulfites.

3. **Fermentation:** The grape juice is allowed to ferment naturally in tanks or barrels. This fermentation process is not complete, and it's halted while the wine is still sweet and low in alcohol (typically around 4-6% alcohol by volume). The resulting wine is cloudy due to the presence of yeast and grape particles.

Characteristics:

- **Sweetness:** Sturm is known for its pronounced sweetness, as the fermentation process is not allowed to continue fully. It has a sweet, fruity flavor, often with notes of apples, pears, and grapes.
- **Fizz:** Sturm is naturally effervescent, and it can have a slight fizz or spritz. This makes it particularly refreshing.
- **Cloudy Appearance:** Sturm is usually cloudy due to the presence of suspended yeast and grape sediment.

Serving and Enjoyment:

- **Chilled:** Sturm is best enjoyed when it's chilled. It's a refreshing beverage, especially on warm autumn days.
- **Seasonal Delight:** Sturm is a seasonal specialty and is typically available for a short period in the early autumn when the new grape harvest is in full swing.
- **Accompaniments:** It's often served with hearty Austrian dishes like Brettljause (a platter of cold cuts, cheese, and bread), sausages, or roasted chestnuts.
- **Limited Shelf Life:** Sturm is a perishable beverage and should be consumed shortly after purchase as

it continues to ferment. It's not suitable for long-term storage.

- **Cultural Tradition:** Enjoying Sturm is a cultural tradition in Austria, and many wine regions host festivals and events to celebrate its release.

- **Varieties:** In addition to the traditional "weißer Sturm" (white Sturm), there's also "roter Sturm" (red Sturm) made from red grape varieties.

Sturm is a unique and delicious autumnal treat that captures the essence of the grape harvest season. If you have the opportunity to visit Austria during the grape harvest season, trying Sturm is a must to experience the local culture and flavors.

Schnapps

Schnapps is a broad category of alcoholic spirits that originated in Germany and Austria, although similar products exist in various forms in many countries. It is known for its strong, clear, and often fruit-flavored nature. Schnapps can range from relatively low-proof liqueurs to high-proof, unaged brandies. Here's an overview of Schnapps:

Production:

1. **Base Ingredient:** Schnapps can be made from various base ingredients, including fruit, herbs, grains, and potatoes.

2. **Fermentation:** For fruit-based Schnapps, the base fruit is crushed, fermented, and then distilled. For grain or potato-based Schnapps, the starches are fermented and then distilled.

3. **Distillation:** The fermented liquid is distilled to increase the alcohol content. Schnapps is typically distilled to a higher proof than many other spirits.

4. **Flavoring:** After distillation, Schnapps can be flavored with a variety of ingredients, including fruit extracts, herbs, spices, and even other spirits. Fruit Schnapps, in particular, are known for their fruity flavors.

Types of Schnapps:

1. **Fruit Schnapps:** These are made from a variety of fruits, including apples, pears, cherries, apricots, and plums. Fruit Schnapps often have a sweet, fruity flavor and can be enjoyed on their own or used as a flavoring in cocktails.

2. **Herbal Schnapps:** These are flavored with a blend of herbs, roots, and botanicals. Herbal Schnapps may have a more complex and bitter flavor profile.

3. **Grain Schnapps:** Made from grains like wheat, rye, or corn, these Schnapps can have a neutral flavor and a higher alcohol content. They are often used as a base spirit in cocktails.

4. **Potato Schnapps:** Made from potatoes, these Schnapps can have a unique, earthy flavor.

Characteristics:

- **Alcohol Content:** Schnapps typically has a higher alcohol content, ranging from 30% to 60% ABV (alcohol by volume), although it can vary.
- **Clarity:** Schnapps is generally clear and colorless, although some fruit varieties may have a slight tint.
- **Flavor:** The flavor of Schnapps varies widely based on the ingredients used. Fruit Schnapps have a pronounced fruit flavor, while herbal Schnapps can have complex herbal and botanical notes.

Consumption:

- **Straight:** Schnapps can be enjoyed straight as a sipping spirit. Fruit Schnapps, in particular, are often served chilled.
- **Cocktails:** Schnapps is used as an ingredient in various cocktails, adding both flavor and alcohol content. It's a common component in drinks like the Appletini and Peppermint Schnapps-based cocktails.
- **Dessert:** Some fruit Schnapps are used as a topping for ice cream or incorporated into desserts.
- **Digestif:** In Austria and Germany, Schnapps is often consumed as a digestif after a meal to aid digestion.

It's important to note that the term "Schnapps" can have different meanings in various countries. In some places, it refers specifically to fruit brandies, while in others, it encompasses a broader category of flavored spirits. The specific characteristics and flavors of Schnapps can vary widely based on the producer and region of origin.

Special Occasion Recipes
Weihnachtsgans (Christmas Goose)

Weihnachtsgans, or Christmas Goose, is a festive and traditional holiday dish enjoyed in Germany, Austria, and other parts of Europe during the Christmas season. It's a hearty and flavorful roast goose dish typically served as the centerpiece of the Christmas dinner table. Here's how to prepare a classic Christmas Goose:

Ingredients:

For the Goose:

- 1 whole goose (approximately 10-12 pounds or 4.5-5.5 kg)
- Salt and freshly ground black pepper
- 2-3 tablespoons vegetable oil or goose fat

For the Stuffing:

- 1-2 onions, finely chopped

- 2-3 apples, peeled, cored, and diced
- 1 cup (150g) dried breadcrumbs
- 1/2 cup (75g) dried cranberries or raisins
- 1 teaspoon dried marjoram
- 1 teaspoon dried thyme
- Salt and freshly ground black pepper to taste
- 1/2 cup (120ml) white wine or water

Instructions:

Preparing the Goose:

1. **Preheat Oven:** Preheat your oven to 350°F (175°C).
2. **Clean the Goose:** Remove any giblets or neck from inside the goose. Rinse the goose inside and out with cold water and pat it dry with paper towels.
3. **Season the Goose:** Season the inside and outside of the goose generously with salt and freshly ground black pepper.
4. **Prepare the Stuffing:** In a large mixing bowl, combine the finely chopped onions, diced apples, dried breadcrumbs, dried cranberries or raisins, dried marjoram, dried thyme, salt, and black pepper. Mix well. You can also add a little white wine or water to moisten the stuffing mixture.
5. **Stuff the Goose:** Stuff the cavity of the goose with the prepared stuffing. Be sure not to overstuff it, as the stuffing will expand during roasting.
6. **Truss the Goose:** To help the goose cook evenly, truss it by tying the legs together with kitchen twine and tucking the wings under the body.

7. **Roast the Goose:** Place the goose, breast-side up, on a roasting rack in a roasting pan. Brush the skin with vegetable oil or goose fat to help it become crispy during roasting.

8. **Roast:** Roast the goose in the preheated oven for about 3 to 3.5 hours, or until the skin is golden brown, and the internal temperature reaches at least 165°F (74°C) when measured in the thickest part of the thigh.

9. **Baste:** During roasting, baste the goose with its own juices or a little additional oil or fat a few times to keep it moist.

10. **Rest:** Once the goose is cooked, remove it from the oven, cover it loosely with aluminum foil, and let it rest for about 20-30 minutes. This allows the juices to redistribute, resulting in a moist and flavorful bird.

11. **Carve and Serve:** Carve the Christmas Goose and serve it with the delicious stuffing and your favorite holiday side dishes, such as red cabbage, dumplings, or roasted potatoes.

Enjoy your festive Weihnachtsgans, a cherished Christmas tradition that brings warmth and flavor to holiday gatherings in Germany, Austria, and beyond.

Osterpinze (Easter Bread)

Osterpinze is a traditional Easter bread from Austria, especially popular in the region of Styria. It's a sweet and slightly spiced bread that's often adorned with a decorative cross or other Easter symbols. Here's how to make this delightful Easter treat:

Ingredients:

For the Dough:

- 4 cups (500g) all-purpose flour
- 1/2 cup (100g) granulated sugar
- 1 packet (7g) active dry yeast
- 1/2 cup (120ml) warm milk
- 1/2 cup (120ml) warm water
- 2 large eggs
- 1/2 cup (113g) unsalted butter, melted
- Zest of 1 lemon

- 1/2 teaspoon ground cinnamon
- 1/4 teaspoon ground nutmeg
- 1/4 teaspoon salt

For the Topping:

- 1 egg yolk, beaten (for egg wash)
- Sliced almonds (for decoration)
- Powdered sugar (for dusting)

Instructions:

1. **Activate the Yeast:** In a small bowl, combine the warm milk, warm water, and a pinch of sugar. Sprinkle the yeast over the mixture, give it a gentle stir, and let it sit for about 10 minutes or until it becomes frothy. This indicates that the yeast is active.

2. **Prepare the Dough:** In a large mixing bowl, combine the flour, granulated sugar, ground cinnamon, ground nutmeg, and salt. Make a well in the center of the dry ingredients.

3. **Mix Wet Ingredients:** In a separate bowl, whisk together the eggs, melted butter, lemon zest, and the activated yeast mixture.

4. **Knead the Dough:** Pour the wet ingredients into the well in the dry ingredients. Stir until a dough forms. Turn the dough out onto a floured surface and knead it for about 10-15 minutes until it becomes smooth and elastic. If the dough is too sticky, you can add a little more flour.

5. **First Rise:** Place the dough in a greased bowl, cover it with a clean kitchen towel, and let it rise in a warm, draft-free place for about 1-2 hours, or until it has doubled in size.

6. **Shape the Osterpinze:** Once the dough has risen, punch it down to remove excess air. Divide it into two equal portions. Shape each portion into a round or oval loaf, and then flatten it slightly.

7. **Decorate:** Using a knife or kitchen scissors, make several decorative cuts on the surface of each loaf. You can create a cross or other Easter-themed designs. Brush the loaves with beaten egg yolk and sprinkle sliced almonds on top.

8. **Second Rise:** Place the decorated loaves on a baking sheet lined with parchment paper. Cover them with a clean kitchen towel and let them rise again for about 30-45 minutes.

9. **Preheat and Bake:** Preheat your oven to 350°F (175°C). Bake the Osterpinze in the preheated oven for 30-35 minutes or until they are golden brown and sound hollow when tapped on the bottom.

10. **Cool and Serve:** Remove the Osterpinze from the oven and let them cool on a wire rack. Once they are completely cooled, dust them with powdered sugar.

11. **Enjoy:** Slice and enjoy your homemade Osterpinze as a sweet and festive Easter treat with family and friends.

Osterpinze is a delightful Easter tradition that combines the flavors of sweet bread with hints of spices and citrus. It's a perfect addition to your Easter celebration, both for its delicious taste and its decorative appeal.

Silvesterkrapfen (New Year's Eve Doughnuts)

Silvesterkrapfen are a delightful Austrian treat traditionally enjoyed on New Year's Eve (Silvester) to celebrate the arrival of the new year. These doughnuts are typically filled with jam or marmalade and dusted with powdered sugar. Here's how to make them:

Ingredients:

For the Dough:

- 2 1/4 cups (280g) all-purpose flour
- 2 1/4 teaspoons (7g) active dry yeast
- 1/4 cup (60ml) lukewarm milk
- 1/4 cup (60ml) lukewarm water
- 2 tablespoons granulated sugar
- 1/4 teaspoon salt
- 1 large egg
- 2 tablespoons unsalted butter, softened

For Frying:

- Vegetable oil for deep frying

For Filling and Garnish:

- Fruit jam or marmalade (e.g., apricot or raspberry)
- Powdered sugar for dusting

Instructions:

Prepare the Dough:

1. **Activate the Yeast:** In a small bowl, combine the lukewarm milk, lukewarm water, and 1 tablespoon of sugar. Sprinkle the yeast over the mixture, give it a gentle stir, and let it sit for about 10 minutes or until it becomes frothy. This indicates that the yeast is active.

2. **Mix Ingredients:** In a large mixing bowl, combine the flour, remaining sugar, and salt. Make a well in the center of the dry ingredients.

3. **Combine Wet Ingredients:** Pour the activated yeast mixture into the well, add the egg, and softened butter. Mix everything together until a dough forms.

4. **Knead the Dough:** Turn the dough out onto a floured surface and knead it for about 5-7 minutes until it becomes smooth and elastic. If the dough is too sticky, you can add a little more flour.

5. **First Rise:** Place the dough in a greased bowl, cover it with a clean kitchen towel, and let it rise in a warm, draft-free place for about 1 hour or until it has doubled in size.

Shape and Fry the Doughnuts:

6. **Roll Out and Cut:** After the first rise, roll out the dough on a floured surface to a thickness of about

1/2 inch (1.3 cm). Use a round cookie cutter or a glass to cut out doughnut shapes. You can also use a smaller cutter to make a hole in the center of each doughnut.

7. **Second Rise:** Place the cut-out doughnuts on a baking sheet lined with parchment paper. Cover them with a clean kitchen towel and let them rise for another 30-45 minutes.

8. **Heat Oil:** In a deep, heavy-bottomed pot, heat vegetable oil to 350°F (175°C) for frying.

9. **Fry:** Carefully place the risen doughnuts into the hot oil, a few at a time, and fry until they are golden brown on both sides, turning them as needed. This should take about 2-3 minutes per side.

10. **Drain and Cool:** Remove the fried doughnuts using a slotted spoon and place them on paper towels to drain any excess oil. Allow them to cool slightly.

Fill and Garnish:

11. **Fill the Doughnuts:** Once the doughnuts are cool enough to handle, use a pastry bag or a small knife to fill them with your favorite fruit jam or marmalade. You can also roll them in powdered sugar or dust powdered sugar on top.

12. **Serve:** Serve your Silvesterkrapfen as a sweet treat to celebrate the New Year!

These delicious Austrian New Year's Eve doughnuts are sure to be a hit with family and friends as you ring in the new year with a sweet and indulgent tradition.

Heiliger Abend Suppe (Christmas Eve Soup)

Heiliger Abend Suppe, or Christmas Eve Soup, is a traditional Austrian soup served on Christmas Eve. It's a comforting and hearty soup that often features a clear broth, root vegetables, and a variety of optional ingredients. Here's a basic recipe for this festive dish:

Ingredients:

For the Soup Base:

- 8 cups (2 liters) beef or vegetable broth
- 1 onion, finely chopped
- 2 carrots, peeled and diced
- 2 celery stalks, diced
- 2 parsnips, peeled and diced
- 2 potatoes, peeled and diced
- 1 leek, sliced (white and light green parts only)
- 2 cloves garlic, minced

- 2 bay leaves
- 1 teaspoon dried thyme
- Salt and freshly ground black pepper, to taste

Optional Ingredients (Choose Based on Your Preferences):

- Sliced mushrooms
- Sliced cooked sausages (such as Vienna sausages or bratwurst)
- Cooked and shredded chicken or turkey
- Cooked dumplings or noodles
- Chopped fresh parsley for garnish
- Lemon wedges for serving

Instructions:

1. **Prepare the Vegetables:** In a large soup pot, heat a little oil over medium heat. Add the chopped onion, celery, carrots, parsnips, and leek. Sauté for about 5 minutes until the vegetables begin to soften.

2. **Add Garlic and Seasonings:** Add the minced garlic, dried thyme, bay leaves, salt, and freshly ground black pepper to the pot. Sauté for another 1-2 minutes until fragrant.

3. **Pour in Broth:** Pour in the beef or vegetable broth, depending on your preference. Bring the mixture to a boil.

4. **Simmer:** Reduce the heat to low, cover the pot, and let the soup simmer for about 20-25 minutes or until the vegetables are tender.

5. **Add Optional Ingredients:** If you're including mushrooms, sausages, chicken or turkey, dumplings,

or noodles, add them to the simmering soup. Cook until they are heated through.

6. **Taste and Adjust:** Taste the soup and adjust the seasoning with salt and pepper if needed.

7. **Remove Bay Leaves:** Remove the bay leaves from the soup.

8. **Serve:** Ladle the Heiliger Abend Suppe into soup bowls. Garnish with chopped fresh parsley and serve with lemon wedges on the side for a burst of citrus flavor.

9. **Enjoy:** Enjoy this warm and comforting Christmas Eve Soup as a festive and nourishing start to your holiday meal.

Heiliger Abend Suppe is a versatile soup that you can customize to your family's preferences by adding or omitting various ingredients. It's a wonderful way to celebrate the Christmas season with a hearty and heartwarming dish.

Osterlamm (Easter Lamb Cake)

Osterlamm, or Easter Lamb Cake, is a traditional German and Austrian dessert that is typically prepared and enjoyed during the Easter season. It is shaped like a lamb, symbolizing the Lamb of God in Christian tradition. This sweet cake is often served as a centerpiece for Easter brunch or dessert. Here's how to make it:

Ingredients:

For the Cake:

- 1 cup (225g) unsalted butter, softened
- 1 cup (200g) granulated sugar
- 4 large eggs
- 2 cups (250g) all-purpose flour
- 2 teaspoons baking powder
- 1/2 cup (120ml) milk
- 1 teaspoon vanilla extract
- Zest of 1 lemon (optional)

For the Coating:

- 1/4 cup (60g) apricot jam or fruit preserves (for glazing)
- Powdered sugar (for dusting)

Equipment:

- Lamb-shaped cake mold (available online or in specialty stores)
- Pastry brush

Instructions:

1. **Preheat the Oven:** Preheat your oven to 350°F (175°C). Grease and flour the lamb-shaped cake mold, making sure to coat it thoroughly to prevent sticking.
2. **Prepare the Batter:** In a mixing bowl, cream together the softened butter and granulated sugar until light and fluffy. This can take about 3-5 minutes with an electric mixer.
3. **Add Eggs:** Add the eggs, one at a time, beating well after each addition.
4. **Combine Dry Ingredients:** In a separate bowl, whisk together the all-purpose flour and baking powder.
5. **Alternate Mixing:** Gradually add the flour mixture to the butter and egg mixture, alternating with the milk, until everything is well combined. Stir in the vanilla extract and lemon zest (if using).
6. **Fill the Mold:** Pour the cake batter into the prepared lamb-shaped cake mold, filling it up to about 2/3 full. Make sure to spread the batter evenly.
7. **Bake:** Place the mold on a baking sheet (to catch any potential drips) and bake in the preheated

oven for approximately 45-50 minutes, or until a toothpick inserted into the center of the cake comes out clean.

8. **Cool:** Allow the cake to cool in the mold for about 10 minutes before carefully removing it from the mold. Place it on a wire rack to cool completely.

9. **Glaze:** Heat the apricot jam or fruit preserves in a small saucepan over low heat until it becomes liquid. Brush the warm glaze over the cooled cake to give it a shiny finish.

10. **Decorate:** You can use powdered sugar to dust the lamb cake for a snowy effect. Additionally, you can add icing or frosting to decorate the lamb's features, such as the eyes, nose, and ears.

11. **Serve:** Place the Osterlamm as a centerpiece on your Easter table and enjoy it as a sweet and symbolic dessert.

The Osterlamm is a cherished Easter tradition that combines delicious cake with a meaningful symbol of the season. It's a delightful treat to share with family and friends during Easter celebrations.

Conclusion
The Enduring Allure of Austrian Cuisine
Austrian cuisine has captivated food enthusiasts worldwide with its rich and diverse flavors, reflecting the country's cultural heritage and regional influences. Rooted in tradition and known for its hearty, comforting dishes, Austrian cuisine continues to hold an enduring allure for both locals and international visitors. Here are some reasons why Austrian cuisine remains so enticing:

1. Historical Significance: Austrian cuisine carries a historical legacy dating back centuries. Influences from the Habsburg Empire, as well as neighboring countries like Hungary, Italy, and the Czech Republic, have left their mark on the culinary landscape. This historical depth adds layers of complexity to Austrian dishes.

2. Regional Diversity: Austria's varied landscapes, from the Alpine regions to the Danube Valley, contribute to the country's diverse cuisine. Each region boasts its own specialties, from hearty mountain fare like Wiener Schnitzel to lighter, Danube-inspired dishes such as fish-based meals.

3. Classic Dishes: Austrian cuisine is celebrated for its classic dishes that have stood the test of time. These include Wiener Schnitzel, Apfelstrudel, and Sachertorte, which have become iconic representations of Austrian culinary culture.

4. Quality Ingredients: Austria's commitment to quality ingredients is evident in its agriculture and farming practices. Fresh, locally sourced ingredients, including dairy products, meats, and seasonal produce, play a pivotal role in creating flavorful and wholesome dishes.

5. Culinary Traditions: Austrian cuisine is steeped in traditions that are passed down through generations. From holiday specialties like Osterlamm to seasonal delicacies like Sturm, these traditions provide a sense of continuity and celebration.

6. Time-Honored Bakeries and Cafés: Vienna, in particular, is renowned for its historic coffeehouses and patisseries. These establishments, such as Café Central and Demel, offer a glimpse into the opulence and elegance of the past, serving delightful cakes, pastries, and coffee concoctions.

7. Balance of Flavors: Austrian cuisine strikes a harmonious balance of flavors, often combining sweet and savory elements in a single dish. The use of spices like paprika, caraway seeds, and marjoram adds depth to the cuisine.

8. Wine Culture: Austria has a burgeoning wine culture, with vineyards producing excellent white wines like Grüner Veltliner and Riesling. These wines pair perfectly with many Austrian dishes and are celebrated internationally.

9. Seasonal Fare: Austrian cuisine is deeply rooted in seasonal eating. The use of fresh ingredients when they are at their peak ensures that dishes are both flavorful and nutritious.

10. Warmth and Hospitality: Austrian cuisine is often enjoyed in the company of family and friends. The warmth and hospitality of Austrian culture make dining an enjoyable and communal experience.

The enduring allure of Austrian cuisine lies in its ability to merge the old with the new, offering a taste of history while adapting to contemporary tastes and trends. Whether you're indulging in a slice of Sachertorte in a Viennese café or savoring the flavors of traditional Alpine fare in a rustic mountain hut, Austrian cuisine continues to enchant and delight, making it a culinary treasure worth exploring.

Encouragement to Explore and Enjoy Austrian Cooking

Exploring and enjoying Austrian cooking is an invitation to embark on a culinary journey filled with rich flavors, time-honored traditions, and a delightful blend of sweet and savory creations. Here's some encouragement to inspire your culinary adventure in Austrian cuisine:

1. **Discover the Classics:** Start by exploring iconic Austrian dishes like Wiener Schnitzel, Apfelstrudel, and Sachertorte. These classics are not only

delicious but also serve as a delicious introduction to the world of Austrian cooking.

2. **Embrace Seasonal Ingredients:** Austrian cuisine places a strong emphasis on using fresh, seasonal ingredients. Embrace the changing seasons and try recipes that feature local produce and flavors unique to each time of year.

3. **Visit Local Markets:** If you have the opportunity, visit local markets in Austria or your own region to source fresh ingredients. You'll find a vibrant array of fruits, vegetables, meats, and artisanal products that can inspire your cooking.

4. **Experiment with Regional Variations:** Austria's diverse regions offer distinct culinary traditions. Experiment with dishes from different parts of the country, such as hearty Alpine fare or lighter Danube-inspired cuisine.

5. **Bake Austrian Delicacies:** Try your hand at baking traditional Austrian pastries and desserts. Whether it's making a perfect strudel pastry or crafting a beautifully decorated Osterlamm, baking can be a fun and rewarding experience.

6. **Explore Austrian Wine:** Pairing Austrian dishes with local wines is a delightful way to enhance your dining experience. Discover the world of Austrian wines, from crisp Grüner Veltliners to elegant Rieslings.

7. **Host Themed Dinners:** Invite friends and family over for themed Austrian dinners. Create a menu featuring multiple courses, including appetizers, mains, and desserts, and enjoy the communal aspect of Austrian dining.

8. **Learn from Experts:** Consider taking a cooking class or seeking guidance from experts in Austrian cuisine. Their knowledge and insights can help you master the techniques and flavors of this culinary tradition.

9. **Celebrate Austrian Holidays:** Embrace Austrian culture by celebrating holidays with traditional dishes. Enjoy Christmas with Osterlamm, Easter with festive lamb cake, and other seasonal specialties.

10. **Share the Joy:** One of the joys of cooking is sharing your creations with others. Invite loved ones to savor your Austrian dishes and share in the experience of discovery.

11. **Document Your Culinary Adventures:** Keep a journal or blog to document your Austrian cooking adventures. Capture your successes, challenges, and memorable moments in the kitchen.

12. **Have Fun:** Above all, remember that cooking should be enjoyable. Don't be afraid to experiment, adapt recipes to your taste, and have fun in the process. The joy of cooking is as important as the end result.

Exploring Austrian cooking allows you to connect with a rich culinary heritage and indulge in the flavors of a country known for its passion for good food. Whether you're a seasoned chef or a novice in the kitchen, Austrian cuisine offers endless opportunities to create, savor, and share memorable meals with loved ones. So, put on your apron, gather your ingredients, and let the enticing aromas and flavors of Austria inspire your culinary journey. Guten Appetit!